The Heart of Wisdom

The Heart of Wisdom

A Philosophy of Spiritual Life

Richard White

ROWMAN & LITTLEFIELD PUBLISHERS, INC.
Lanham • Boulder • New York • Toronto • Plymouth, UK

Published by Rowman & Littlefield Publishers, Inc.
A wholly owned subsidiary of The Rowman & Littlefield Publishing Group, Inc.
4501 Forbes Boulevard, Suite 200, Lanham, Maryland 20706
www.rowman.com

10 Thornbury Road, Plymouth PL6 7PP, United Kingdom

British Library Cataloguing in Publication Information Available

Library of Congress Cataloging-in-Publication Data

White, Richard J. (Richard John), 1956–
The heart of wisdom : a philosophy of spiritual life / Richard White.
p. cm.
Includes bibliographical references and index.
ISBN 978-1-4422-2116-1 (cloth : alk. paper) — ISBN 978-1-4422-2117-8 (electronic)
1. Spiritual life. 2. Philosophy and religion. 3. Philosophical theology. I. Title.
BL624.W465 2013
204.01—dc23
2012038786

♾™ The paper used in this publication meets the minimum requirements of
American National Standard for Information Sciences Permanence of Paper for
Printed Library Materials, ANSI/NISO Z39.48-1992.

Printed in the United States of America

Contents

Acknowledgments

I am very grateful for the support and encouragement of all my friends and colleagues at Creighton University. Also, to all my students over the past few years who challenged me to refine "the way of philosophy" that is described in this book. I owe so much to Clarinda who helped me to think more deeply about spirituality, and who showed me what it means to live a spiritual life. Thanks to Adam for finding his own way.

This book is dedicated to the memory of my mother, Margaret White, who understood the importance of these ideas.

An earlier version of chapter 1 was published as "Levinas, the Philosophy of Suffering and the Ethics of Compassion" in *The Heythrop Journal* (vol. 53, no. 1, January 2012). A part of chapter 4 was published as "Lyotard and Posthuman Possibilities" in *Philosophy Today* (vol. 50, no. 2, Summer 2006). Thanks to the editors of both journals for permission to include this material.

Introduction

What is spirituality, and what does it mean to live a spiritual life? For many people, "spirituality" is still a vague idea that needs some clarification. We are told that philosophy can help. But how can philosophy make sense of spirituality if its goal is just to give a *critique* of spiritual ideas? Placing spirituality within rational parameters only seems to undermine it, for "the spiritual" is something that appears to transcend reason. It cannot be reduced to concepts, and it is more than the sum of its parts. Modern philosophers and other thinkers—including Hume, Marx, and Freud—have been very suspicious of spiritual themes, and it follows that "the way of philosophy" is not an obvious spiritual path. The relationship between spirituality and religion is also fraught with complexity. When some people talk about their spiritual life they just mean their religious values and commitments, while for others, the fixed practices of traditional religion are a hindrance to their spiritual growth. For some, spirituality is all about cultivating the divine spark within; but not all spiritual seekers have religious beliefs, and others are quite skeptical of religion and every form of divinity. All of which suggests that spirituality is a difficult theme to determine, and yet it speaks to us as one of the most important values in life.

In recent years, explicitly spiritual concerns have become more prominent than before. Many people now enjoy a comfortable lifestyle with abundant material possessions, but they find that their lives are impoverished; their lives do not possess the significance they wish they had, and so they search for a spiritual meaning. This suggests that "spirituality" is a kind of refuge from everyday existence and that the spiritual world is just the opposite of the material world we belong to. It also implies that spirituality is a kind of luxury. According to the hierarchy of human needs, we are bound to satisfy the need for food, shelter, and clothing, even our desire for a certain standard of living, before we can think about the more exalted need for a meaningful life—which is more than just being materially successful. On the other hand, many poor people are able to live spiritually significant lives because they are not distracted by the pursuit of wealth. Gandhi's personal possessions were limited to his food bowl, his clothes, and his glasses; there are many others like him—monks, nuns, hermits, and recluses of all kinds—who *choose* a life of poverty because it is spiritually enhancing. We may not be able to live without material goods, but spiritual goods are those that make life meaningful. In this respect, spirituality is not a luxury or a secondary concern. In fact, it is among the most important things to consider when we think about what makes life worth living—and this is a *philosophical* question.

So to what extent are questions about spirituality really open to philosophical reflection? In the first part of this introduction, I will suggest three different ways of thinking about our spiritual life from a philosophical point of view. First, as we have already seen, spirituality can be understood as *the opposite of selfish materialism*: to live a spiritual life means turning away from the ordinary concerns of everyday life—including personal ambition or wealth—to concentrate on matters of ultimate concern. The second suggestion is that spirituality can be viewed as *a journey toward fulfillment and enlightenment*, and as such it involves the quest for a more meaningful life. Lastly, spirituality may also be looked at in terms of *an encounter with ultimate reality and meaning*—however this is finally understood—for it involves grasping the deeper truth about the world. Of course, all three aspects are interrelated and are only separated for the sake of analysis. They are not three separate features of spiritual life, but three different perspectives on the same thing which help to illuminate it more completely. Much of the following discussion depends upon a *phenomenological* account of our experience as we apprehend it. We must remain critical; but at the same time, we experience the world as a meaningful place, and spiritual realities—including nature, beauty, and truth—are just as real to us as any of our moral duties or our personal feelings.

UNDERSTANDING SPIRITUALITY

First, spiritual concerns can be defined in opposition to material concerns. Consider a life that was focused on accumulating wealth and status or power over others. Such a life would be completely self-absorbed. One could never step back from such a life to think about the needs of others, and one would have no sense of one's ultimate connection to the rest of the world. A selfish life disdains connection, and it is unconcerned with matters of ultimate concern. Such a life is lacking in spiritual reflection, and it may be criticized for the refusal to go beyond what is immediately in front of it. Now consider a life focused on spiritual concerns—which include living a meaningful life and grasping higher realities. This life would not be selfish in any ordinary sense, but neither would it be "useful" or open to any kind of objective measurement. This does not mean that spirituality is "otherworldly." The impulse to spirituality includes a strong desire to make sense out of *this* world, using contemplation, meditation, and other practices to experience our fundamental connection to nature, the community of human existence, and the cosmos itself. Many poets, scientists, and philosophers have a sense of the sacred character of *this* life that they try to convey; and even Nietzsche, the philosopher who announces "the death of God," affirms the value of earthly life against traditional religion, which has frequently undermined it. For if this life is just a "vale of tears" there is no pressing need to understand its ultimate significance. Nietzsche denies that the bad things in life constitute an objection to the world's existence, and through his prophet Zarathustra, he proclaims that *this* world is sacred:

> The world is deep,
> Deeper than day had been aware.
> Deep is its woe;
> Joy—deeper yet than agony:
> Woe implores: Go!
> But all joy wants eternity—
> Wants deep, wants deep eternity."[1]

Putting this point differently, we can say that spirituality is concerned with the sacred, for it dwells on those experiences in which life seems to justify itself. These might be sublime or momentous experiences as when we are confronted by the vast ocean, the powerful waterfall, or the immensity of space. But even smaller moments in life including "random acts of human kindness" can be astonishing. Of course, the sacred can be viewed as another realm of being entirely, like "heaven," but the sacred may also be discovered in the ordinary, everyday aspects of this life, such as breathing, walking, or feeling the warmth of sunlight. These are sometimes regarded as purely physical sensations, but they can also have the same spiritual significance that we have described. In this respect, spirituality may be the antidote to crass materialism and selfish preoccupations, but it is not merely escapism to another realm of being. Although spirituality is often contrasted with the material world, it also belongs to this world as part of its deepest reality and truth.

The second perspective on spirituality is to think of it in terms of a personal journey toward self-fulfillment and connection with the deepest values that underlie our existence. In this respect, spirituality is best understood as part of a personal quest that leads each individual toward a more meaningful life. Spiritual values are those that concern whatever makes life valuable. They are not narcissistic or self-involved, and the spiritual quest involves the achievement of wisdom as well as self-understanding. Clearly, the underlying assumption here is the absolute trust that this life *is* significant and meaningful and that the individual search for meaning will confirm and strengthen this basic belief.

The various world religions offer spiritual paths that are ready-made for their adherents, but these established views may not be useful for everyone. Likewise, morality is crucial, and it is almost certainly a necessary condition for authentic spirituality, but it is not the same as authentic spirituality. A spiritual value can be a religious value and a spiritual value can be a moral value. But there are plenty of spiritual values that are neither religious nor moral, including art, music, nature, and truth. Also, religion and morality are only *spiritually* relevant insofar as they advance the life of the individual and make it worth living. Duty, when experienced as a crushing burden, would not be a spiritual value, but when experienced as devotion to family and friends, it may enable me to live a more meaningful life than if I stay self-absorbed or absent. Spiritual life, then, involves challenging the ordinary values that we live by, not rejecting them out of hand, but determining the extent of their validity. It involves searching for the truth about the world through philosophy, the appreciation of nature, literature, and other forms of spiritual inquiry, including music, sacred texts, and attunement to physical well-being. It also involves the cultivation of spiritual attitudes such as forgiveness, gratitude, and generosity, for such attitudes open the individual up to the sheer abundance of life and release her from the isolation of subjective self-involvement.

The famous story of the cave in Plato's *Republic* epitomizes the spiritual quest in the context of philosophical reflection. In this story, Plato describes the human condition—we are like prisoners in a cave, chained to a bench in such a way that we can only look at things that are immediately in front of us.

> See human beings as though they were in an underground cave-like dwelling with its entrance, a long one, open to the light across the whole width of the cave. They are in it from childhood with their legs and necks in bonds so that they are fixed, seeing only in front of them, unable because of the bond to turn their heads all the way around. The light is from a fire burning far above and behind them. Between the fire and the prisoners there is a road above, along which see a wall, built like the partitions puppet-handlers set in front of the human beings and over which they show the puppets.[2]

The cave is the spiritual ignorance that we are born into; the chains are the prejudices and received ideas that we inherit from those who have preceded us, and the images on the wall of the cave are the ordinary delusions of everyday life—power, money, and fame—that we spend much of our lives pursuing. One man is freed from his chains and explores what the cave is really like. He sees the fire that casts the shadows, and eventually the sun outside of the cave, which in this story is the source of all light and Being. But after he experiences the blissful happiness of connection with the truth of things, he returns to the cave because he feels compelled to help others make the same spiritual journey that he has just made. The prisoners laugh at him but he refuses to be silent, and because he threatens all of their fixed ideas about the world, and what they think is really important, it is said that they would do violence to him if they could.

Of course, there are many ways to interpret the story of the cave. First of all, it tells the story of Socrates, who called established truths into question and pursued the underlying truth of the world. Socrates was put to death for his attempt to awaken others to such questions of ultimate concern—How should I live? And what is the nature of the good life? Less specifically, the story of the cave describes the spiritual journey of someone who is dissatisfied with the conventional wisdom of society and its emphasis on what is supposed to be *here* and *now*. The spiritual journey that Plato describes has two parts: First, there is a movement of personal liberation, and second, there is the return to the cave in order to help others—and these two parts are the necessary aspects of any authentic spiritual quest. The spiritual journey of the individual is fundamental, but without the return to the cave and the willingness to help others with *their* journey, it remains self-involved. Often, people complain that conventional spirituality has become narcissistic and self-indulgent. Spirituality is big business now, and the focus on New Age forms of self-cultivation seems to undermine any sense of our ultimate connection to the world or to others. This is a reasonable criticism to make, but it ignores the fact that any authentic spiritual enlightenment seems to touch the ultimate reality that supports us all; and to experience this reality is to participate in the fundamental generosity of life. This is not just an *intellectual* achievement, but something that inspires gratitude and love on the part of the seeker, and so it naturally results in caring for others and concern for *their* well-being.

This brings us to the third perspective on spirituality. From one standpoint, the cultivation of the self through spiritual practices such as meditation, fasting, and prayer leads to an intensification of the life of the individual that appears to be self-involved. But another way of thinking about this is to see these spiritual exercises as a training in self-overcoming, or a movement away from the self-preoccupation that characterizes our everyday life. In Buddhism, for example, there are exercises for cultivating compassion, which promote a sense of connection to the rest of the world. In the practice of *tonglen* we imagine ourselves breathing in the sufferings of others as if they were a noxious cloud; then we think of ourselves breathing out the pure air that gives them healing and relief. The Buddhist nun, Pema Chödrön, describes the essence of this practice: "We breathe in what is painful and unwanted with the sincere wish that we and others could be free of suffering. As we do so, we drop the storyline that goes along with the pain and feel the underlying energy. We completely open our hearts and minds to whatever arises. Exhaling, we send out relief from the pain with the intention that we and others be happy."[3] Spiritual practices, including *tonglen*, meditation, prayer, and music, can act as a catalyst for inner transformation and growth. Through the practice of *tonglen*, for example, it becomes possible to experience our community with all sentient beings, and this undermines our sense of ourselves as completely separate individuals.

Thus while the spiritual person is committed to spiritual growth as an essential goal, spiritual life actually involves self-overcoming rather than self-preoccupation. And it leads to an encounter with the world in which we experience a sense of our place in the "big picture" of things. In early Indian philosophical thought, the student is taught by his spiritual guide, or guru, to accept the very limited and secondary character of his own separate existence. In the *Chandogya Upanishad*, the sage Uddalaka addresses his son Shvetaketu, and tells him that he is one with ultimate reality or Brahman:

> As the rivers flowing east and west
> Merge in the sea and become one with it,
> Forgetting they were ever separate rivers,
> So do all creatures lose their separateness
> When they emerge at last into pure Being.
> There is nothing that does not come from him.
> Of everything he is the inmost Self.
> He is the truth; he is Self supreme.
> You are that, Shvetaketu; you are that.[4]

In a profound sense, which is open to spiritual exploration, our underlying Self (or Atman) is held to be equivalent to Brahman, or the basic reality that underlies everything that is. Notice, however, that this is not something to be grasped intellectually as if it were the conclusion to an argument; it is rather the *experience* of a reality that cannot be denied: "You are that, Shvetaketu. You are that." In other words, spirituality in an important sense seems to involve the overcoming of the ego since it leads us to identify with the ultimate truth of the world, as something we must affirm and celebrate for its own sake.

This means that the highest goal of spiritual enlightenment may actually be the withdrawal of the self—not the celebration of the self as some kind of spiritual superman, but the overcoming of the self as a completely separate, self-involved being. This is certainly the case with Asian spiritual traditions such as Hinduism and Buddhism. As the New Age writer Carter Phipps puts it,

> Enlightenment equals ego death. For millennia this equation has held true. While the term "ego," meaning "I" in Latin, is obviously a relatively recent addition to the English lexicon, just about every major enlightenment teaching in the world has long held that the highest goal of spiritual and indeed human life lies in the renunciation, rejection and, ultimately, the death of the need to hold on to a separate, self-centered existence.[5]

Another way of thinking about this would be to say that spirituality involves our finite relation to the infinite, or our relative apprehension of that which is absolute. And while this could derive from a traditional religious experience, it could also come from an exceptional experience of nature, music, beauty, or even "the truth." Through such an experience we encounter a profound reality that we are usually unaware of. This reality holds us and gives us a sense of belonging to something that is inherently meaningful, and for as long as it lasts we are not concerned about our own selfish goals and projects. The ego is no longer important. A spiritual person is someone who is attuned to this kind of experience and who lives her life in mindful awareness of it. But someone who is not particularly spiritual may be unable to relate to these kinds of considerations.

Our preliminary discussion of spiritual life has identified three different aspects or points of concern that help to define spirituality and specify its scope: the spiritual is that which can be distinguished from the material (or the materialistic) and that which is purely selfish; the spiritual is an individual journey toward personal fulfillment and a more meaningful life; and the spiritual is the withdrawal of the self in its encounter with ultimate reality, however this is finally understood.

Now that we have laid out this basic ground, we can go on to consider some of the most significant ways in which the practice of philosophy can illuminate spirituality and the forms of spiritual life. Spirituality is the heart of wisdom because it is the affective core of intellectual understanding. It moves us at the deepest level of who we are and it expresses the ultimate truth concerning human life. At the same time, *philosophy* is viewed as the most foundational of all the disciplines—Descartes called it the queen of the sciences—because it asks the most fundamental questions: What is being? Why is there something rather than nothing? And what is the meaning of life? In this respect, philosophy is also at the heart of wisdom, and we would expect that philosophy would have something to say about spirituality and the nature of an authentic spiritual life.

PHILOSOPHY AS A WAY OF LIFE

For ancient philosophers, including Socrates, the Stoics, Epicureans, and Skeptics, philosophy was not just an intellectual pursuit; it was also a way of life that promised moral and spiritual fulfillment for its practitioners. The practice of philosophy included meditation, self-discipline, and other spiritual exercises; it involved living wisely and well and overcoming the fear of death. It also used a variety of spiritual exercises to challenge received ideas about human life. For example, one goal was to remove "false" values such as wealth, pleasure, and glory, and to turn toward the true values of "virtue, contemplation, a simple life-style, and the simple happiness of existing."[6] And this is why philosophers were ridiculed, and even executed in the case of Socrates, for their existence was a challenge to the non-philosophical life.

For the most part, we have ignored or forgotten this aspect of ancient philosophical traditions, but in recent years, writers such as Pierre Hadot and Michel Foucault have sought to recover it from oblivion. The ancient schools of philosophy, like the wisdom traditions of the East—Buddhism, Confucianism, and Taoism, etc.—all focused on the spiritual well-being of their practitioners. As Hadot puts it, for the ancient writers, "philosophy was a method of spiritual progress which demanded a radical conversion and transformation of the individual's way of being."[7] Philosophy was not an intellectual abstraction, but consisted in the art of living. It raised the individual "from an inauthentic condition of life, darkened by unconsciousness and harassed by worry, to an authentic state of life, in which he attains self-consciousness, an exact vision of the world, inner peace and freedom."[8] Each of the different philosophical schools—Stoic, Platonic, Epicurean, Aristotelian—had its own therapeutic method, but for all of them, the final goal was a profound transformation of the individual's mode of seeing and being, and the overcoming of anguish:

> The philosophical school . . . corresponds, above all, to the choice of a certain way of life and existential option which demands from the individual a total change of lifestyle, a conversion of one's entire being, and ultimately a certain desire to be and to live in a certain way. This existential option, in turn, implies a certain vision of the world, and the task of philosophical discourse will therefore be to reveal and rationally justify this existential option, as well as this representation of the world.[9]

In the modern age, philosophy has become identified with critical thinking and the solution of conceptual puzzles. It is not a threat to anyone. "Our academic thinkers are not dangerous," Nietzsche complains, "for their thoughts grow as peacefully out of tradition as any tree ever bore its apples; they cause no alarm; they remove nothing from its hinges; and of all their art and aims there could be said what Diogenes said when someone praised a philosopher in his presence: 'How can he be considered great, since he has been a philosopher for so long and has never yet *disturbed* anybody?'"[10] Since the time of the ancients, very little has been written on the relationship between philosophy and living a spiritual life. Obviously, there are those philosophers who write on spiritual issues, including suffering, compassion, and forgiveness. But I am unaware of any systematic discussion of spiritual life from a philosophical standpoint that uses critical reflection to illuminate spiritual ideas.

All of which suggests that philosophy has fallen away from its original insight and purpose. The ancient philosophers understood that philosophy is about how to live, and they were preoccupied with spiritual themes and questions, including how we should deal with suffering, how to face death, and what the meaning of life is. Modern philosophers have been less interested in these questions, but they are inherent to philosophy, and there is every reason to think that philosophers may *recover* their understanding of such perennial themes and the sense in which philosophy involves joy in belonging to the truth. Indeed, philosophers in the continental tradition, beginning with Hegel, Kierkegaard, and Nietzsche, and more recently, Heidegger, Levinas, and Derrida, have returned to these fundamental issues which had previously been ignored or considered too subjective or emotional. For this reason, the perspectives and examples used in this book will be drawn primarily from ancient philosophical traditions, including Stoicism and Aristotle; from recent continental philosophy, including Nietzsche, Levinas, Derrida, and Lyotard; and the wisdom traditions of Asia, such as Buddhism and the Vedanta philosophy of India. Spiritual themes, including the very idea of "ultimate reality and meaning," may seem impossibly vague to some contemporary philosophers; but "ultimate reality" remains a guiding idea and it would be foolish to reject it out of hand. It seems clear that philosophy and spirituality are very closely related and enhance each other and that spiritual questions are amenable to philosophical reflection.

AN OUTLINE OF SPIRITUAL UNDERSTANDING

This volume offers a philosophy of spiritual life that covers spiritual issues in a systematic way. Of course, this is only one of several paths that could be taken to explore the truth of spirituality, and it is not meant to be definitive or exclusive. Understanding spiritual life requires critical thinking about forgiveness, generosity, and suffering, but it also requires the *imaginative* leap of philosophy to show the connections between different areas of experience which are usually kept separate from each other. It cannot be denied that some authors in the contemporary spiritual tradition offer keen insights into human life. Writers such as the Dalai Lama, Thomas Moore, and Pema Chödrön give spiritual advice that is helpful and relevant. But at the same time, many other New Age writers have muddled ideas about the soul and the spirit, and their claims are not well-founded. The critical reflection of philosophy helps us to scrutinize spiritual claims and arguments. But the goal of *this* work is to articulate a philosophy of spiritual life by examining important spiritual themes, beginning with suffering and ending with joy.

This book dwells on philosophical issues, but it is intended for all intelligent readers who are concerned with spirituality as a significant part of life. It does not affirm the position of the skeptic or the "true believer." In the chapters that follow, I will consider a variety of different spiritual perspectives, including Buddhism, Christianity, Stoicism, and even the radical atheism of a thinker like Nietzsche. But I will not affirm (or reject) any religious or metaphysical claims. "Spirituality" is a basic category of human experience, and while our religious beliefs certainly shape our spiritual lives, it is also the case that spiritual themes can be separated from their metaphysical context and appreciated for their own sake. I will return to this issue at the end of the book, but for now I will propose that regardless of our religious beliefs—or lack of them—we can always experience moral and spiritual growth by coming to grips with different spiritual perspectives, including those that may be associated with a tradition other than our own. By focusing on some recurrent themes of spiritual life—especially those that are open to philosophical refection—we reach a more complete view of spirituality as a form of life.

This book is by no means a complete account of spirituality, and it has nothing to say about the occult or New Age wisdom that probes alternative realities. Instead, it shows how spiritual life may be grasped in terms of three main divisions which can be described as the *passive*, the *active*, and the *reflective* moments of spirituality. These divisions are abstractions, but they are distinguished here for the sake of analysis and clarification. Each chapter will explore a different spiritual theme, and focus on the work of *spiritual* philosophers, including the Stoics, Levinas, Aquinas, Derrida, the Vedanta philosophers, Nietzsche, Lyotard, and the Dalai Lama. The "religious" philosophers are well-represented, but so is Nietzsche, who offers the possibility of spirituality without God.

We will begin with *suffering,* said to be the beginning of spiritual life, for without suffering there would be no question of the goodness of life, and there would be nothing that cries out for reflection and understanding. As the philosopher Emmanuel Levinas notes, in both physical and spiritual suffering we are pinned down by life: Suffering hurts, and as much as we want to, we cannot just remove ourselves by thinking about something else. Stoicism, Christianity, and Buddhism represent different attempts to deal with the problem of suffering, which seems to form an objection to life itself. In the second chapter, *compassion* is grasped as the most authentic response to suffering, and following Buddhist (and Christian) teachings, we can see how compassion entails profound spiritual wisdom. This chapter pays particular attention to the Dalai Lama's philosophy of compassion as well as the *negative* response to compassion that characterizes one strain of Western philosophy. Both suffering and compassion belong to the passive side of human experience in so far as they are forms of impotence, receptivity, and response. But in the case of compassion, being open to the suffering of others is also the pre-condition for an active spiritual life.

Next, the discussion of *generosity* clarifies the active dimension of spirituality because individual acts of generosity seem to reflect the ultimate generosity of the universe. Such acts are not required; they go beyond the horizon of moral obligation, and they are a celebration of life itself. We can give up our property; but even more astonishing is the fact that we may also give up our lives, and true generosity is found in sacrifice and caring for others. Love is a form of generosity, and the Bible says, "Greater love hath no man than this that a man lay down his life for his friends."[11] The next chapter, on *forgiveness* will show in a more concrete way how such a gift enhances our own spiritual life and the lives of others. As Jacques Derrida points out, true forgiveness—which involves forgiving what should be *unforgivable*—is an act of freedom and a new beginning which renews the world that we belong to. And just as suffering involves the intensification of the self and the experience of its objectification, so generosity—and especially forgiveness—implies freedom *from* the self and a fundamental orientation *toward* others.

Reverence describes the point at which spiritual life becomes reflectively self-conscious. Reverence is neither passive nor active; it is not to be understood in terms of self-absorption or self-overcoming, for it is a contemplative and self-conscious identification with "higher" realities. Reverence is restraint and willing not to will. It is associated with respect and religious contemplation, and it attempts to encounter the sacred dimension of the world without dominating or appropriating it, and without being overwhelmed by it. Nietzsche describes such an attitude as the key to spiritual life itself: "Learning to *see*—accustoming the eye to calmness, to patience, to letting things come up to it; postponing judgment, learning to go around and grasp each individual case from all sides. That is the *first* preliminary schooling for spirituality."[12] More recent thinkers, such as Buber, Lyotard, and Luce Irigaray, help to clarify the nature of reverence as a basic spiritual attitude. They dwell, in particular, on the authentic relation between self and other— where this "other" is another person, the natural world, or even philosophy itself.

After reverence, which is thoughtful and calm, the final chapter describes *joy* as the supreme spiritual emotion which expresses the exuberance of spiritual connection and all the gratitude we are bound to feel for being alive. Of course, we should be suspicious of mindless joy which refuses to reflect on its own conditions, but joy is also a privileged emotion insofar as it discloses the ultimate reality of the world and our sense of belonging to it. The earliest Indian philosophers, Stoics, and Zen Buddhists have sought to articulate this experience of joy as the fulfillment of spiritual life. They are in agreement that it is not a mindless, "blissed-out" feeling of total self-absorption, but an expression of complete attunement with the universe itself. To be in touch with "ultimate reality," whether this is construed as nirvana or the depth of God's love, inspires joy; and significantly, such joy is more often than not a characteristic of the most spiritually accomplished people, including Gandhi and the Dalai Lama.

The discussion that begins with suffering therefore culminates with its opposite, joy, and in this way the whole gamut of spiritual experience is described, not in detail, but in terms of its overall structure and its three basic divisions, passive, active, and reflective. There are many paths through spiritual life, and many different ways to achieve spiritual awareness and centeredness, including yoga, alternative medicine, meditation, and prayer. This book offers "the way of philosophy," or at least *a* way of philosophy which focuses on different spiritual attitudes in the order of their emergence at the conceptual or experiential level. This particular way of philosophy, which looks to the heart of wisdom, supplements other spiritual practices instead of criticizing or rejecting them. It seeks to cultivate spirituality through reflective meditation on each of the spiritual themes discussed; and it encourages spiritual virtues, including compassion, generosity, forgiveness, and reverence, by focusing on *practical* reflection and response.

Chapter One

Suffering

Suffering is the origin of spiritual life, for without the experience of pain or disappointment, frustration or destitution, we could not know all the limitations of individual existence which call our being into question and provoke a reflective response: Why am I suffering? Why is this happening to me? And what have I done to deserve this? Such questions are unavoidable in any life and they lead us to make sense of things by framing our experience within the context of a spiritual reality which is held to be the truth of the physical world. Thus, we cope with our suffering and put it in its place by cultivating our attunement to the spiritual order. In this way, suffering may become a meaningful experience or a necessary evil that promotes individual flourishing and growth. It is no longer the abyss of meaning that renders life null and void.

What is true at the level of the individual is also true of philosophy and religion in general. Some thinkers, including Plato and Aristotle, have argued that philosophy begins with a sense of wonder, for without a feeling of astonishment about the world there would be no impulse to try to make sense of things. More recently, Martin Heidegger argued that the fundamental question of philosophy should be, Why is there something rather than nothing? But suffering engages thought at a much deeper level. We may contemplate the existence of the universe with surprise and wonder, but in suffering, we are pinned down by the world and we cannot escape from ourselves. And as soon as we *can* step back from what is happening to us, we become preoccupied with the need to reflect upon our present misery, to make sense of it, and to explain it, even if we cannot justify it once and for all. Does all suffering have a meaning? Do bad things really happen to good people? Or is the universe ultimately absurd? This is the impulse that provokes both philosophy and religion.

Among the ancient philosophers, the Stoics and Epicureans thought of suffering as the most significant problem of life. For example, the Epicureans lived together in small communities of friends; they deliberately avoided public life and devoted themselves to modest pursuits, like tending their gardens. In all of this, their goal was to avoid suffering and to live a quiet, happy life. According to Epicurus, the practice of philosophy was supposed to overcome the suffering of existence. As he comments in a famous passage, "Empty are the words of that philosopher who offers therapy for no human suffering. Just as there is no use in medical expertise if it does not give therapy for bodily diseases, so too there is no use in philosophy if it does not expel the suffering of the soul."[1] For Epicurus and his followers, the goal of life was to minimize suffering and displeasure of every kind. Hence their argument that it is unreasonable to fear death because death is not an issue when we are still alive, and when we are dead we no longer exist to care about it. The Stoics also focused on suffering by arguing that pain and suffering—along with pleasure—are in themselves neither good nor bad things, but "indifferents," and so the proper attitude to them should be one of indifference. But as we will see in what follows, such a rational response to the problem of suffering assumes the possibility of complete self-mastery, and this would be astonishing since our response to suffering is to a great extent beyond our control.

Religion is also said to begin with the need for an explanation. How did the universe get here? Who created the world, and what is the purpose of my life? Sometimes we say that religion derives from the need for protection from all the perils of human existence and the desire for personal survival in a life that continues after death. Once again, however, it probably makes more sense to say that the impulse to religion, like the impulse to philosophy, is an attempt to make sense of the problem of suffering.

According to Christianity, we are born with original sin, and we are so wretched that only the suffering and sacrifice of God can redeem us. Jesus Christ is the saviour who takes away our sins. Through the crucifixion he experiences absolute suffering, but through the resurrection he shows that suffering and death are only limited truths, and by patiently enduring our own sufferings we can identify with Christ. Thus, in his *First Letter*, Peter commiserates with all of those who suffer persecution: "My dear friends, do not be bewildered by the fiery ordeal that is upon you, as though it were something extraordinary. It gives you a share in Christ's sufferings, and that is cause for joy; and when his glory is revealed, your joy will be triumphant."[2] Through identification with Christ, our own suffering gains a positive meaning. In other religions, including Islam and Judaism, suffering is more routinely regarded as a punishment or a test—witness the story of Job (who is Ayyub in the Koran). But here again, the sense of a punishment or a test redeems suffering by reframing it as a meaningful experience within the context of God's well-ordered universe.

Finally, in Buddhism, Siddhartha Gautama begins his mission in the world to overcome the problem of suffering and to release people from their dissatisfaction with life. After his enlightenment, the Buddha teaches the four Noble truths—that life is suffering; that suffering derives from a desperate attachment to other people and things; that the way out of suffering is by cultivating non-attachment; and that this is to be achieved through the eightfold path, which includes correct ethics, meditation, and wisdom. In the Mahayana tradition of Buddhism, emphasis is placed on the bodhisattva, or the saint, who vows identification with all beings who suffer, and refuses to enter nirvana until all other beings have been released from their sufferings. In *The Way of the Bodhisattva,* Shantideva concludes his account with the bodhisattva's vow:

> And now as long as space endures,
> As long as there are beings to be found,
> May I continue likewise to remain
> To drive away the sorrows of the world.
> The pains and sorrows of all wandering beings—
>   May they ripen wholly on myself.
> And may the virtuous company of bodhisattvas
> Bring about the happiness of beings.[3]

Here, in Buddhism, as in other ancient philosophies and religions, it is the experience of suffering that inaugurates spiritual life. In what follows, however, we look more closely at *contemporary* philosophical responses to physical and emotional suffering, starting with the work of Emmanuel Levinas and others who write on torture and the extremity of physical and emotional anguish.

To what extent can suffering become a meaningful experience? And can suffering ever be justified—whether now or later—in terms of "spiritual development" or the achievement of some common good? On the face of it, suffering is an inherently negative experience and it seems contradictory to look for a meaning in something that appears to *take away* meaning. Even so, Nietzsche writes famously that "what does not destroy me makes me stronger," and there is wisdom in Kierkegaard's claim that suffering is the necessary condition for all spiritual growth—as one of his *Upbuilding Discourses* proclaims: "The Joy of It, That the School of Sufferings Educates for Eternity."[4] Now it may be the case that some kinds of *spiritual* suffering can be viewed in this way—the various forms of despair, guilt, bad conscience, anguish, and loneliness that eventually lead to a deeper level of insight and self-understanding. But set against this would be the devastating grief that we associate with the death of loved ones and the trauma of separation or abuse which undermines the meaning of life instead of affirming it. If we consider *physical* suffering, a similar distinction can be made: some physical pain can be useful in letting us know our body has been damaged; or it can be necessary, like a painkilling injection, just to avoid more suffering in the future. But there comes a point when physical suffering is so extreme or on such a massive scale that any attempt to justify it in terms of God's plan or the march of progress is morally repugnant, and the worst exercise of (philosophical) bad faith.

"Theodicy" is the common term for the justification of God's goodness in the face of the existence of evil—when we say that it is all part of God's plan. But the philosopher Emmanuel Levinas calls it a "scandal" *whenever* extreme suffering is justified in terms of some higher good. In light of the Holocaust and other atrocities of the twentieth century, Levinas claims that any kind of theodicy—whether this is a natural or supernatural justification of suffering—is evil in itself: for the willingness to *justify* the suffering of other people is what allows an outrage such as the Holocaust to happen in the first place. In this respect, Levinas goes so far as to claim that "the justification of the neighbour's pain is certainly the source of all immorality."[5] Richard Cohen describes the problem in traditional theological language: "Since God wills all things, God willed the Holocaust. Because all things willed by God are good, the Holocaust too was good. Not just that good comes from the Holocaust, but that the Holocaust itself was good, as repentance, sacrifice, purification, sign, redemption, punishment, perhaps all of these, but ultimately good in itself."[6] This chapter is not about "the problem of theodicy," but it is an attempt to say something about the philosophical significance of suffering.

There are three questions that will guide this inquiry. First is the question concerning the *nature* of suffering: What is suffering and how is it to be described? For Levinas, suffering is viewed as radical passivity and a pure *undergoing* which shatters my capacity for ordering the world. In suffering, he writes, "there is an absence of all refuge. It is the fact of being directly exposed to being. It is made up of the impossibility of fleeing or retreating. The whole acuity of suffering lies in this impossibility of retreat. It is the fact of being backed up against life and being. In this sense suffering is the impossibility of nothingness."[7] Levinas's account of suffering is profoundly insightful, but his philosophical language is difficult, and we must clarify these claims. The second question concerns the *meaning* of suffering: Can such (extreme) suffering ever be viewed as meaningful in terms of the big picture it belongs to? Is it "useful" suffering, or do we have to say that it is "useless"? And leaving aside the suffering of others, what about the significance of my own pain? The third question concerns the *response* to suffering: What should the proper reaction to suffering be? Some thinkers, including Job's friends, respond to suffering with theodicy, for they refuse to accept that God would ever allow anything to happen without good reason. Some thinkers, such as the Stoics, avoid suffering by insisting that nothing can hurt us unless we allow it to, which assumes the (unlikely) possibility of complete self-mastery. Others, including those in the Buddhist tradition, argue that compassion is the supreme virtue and it must be cultivated as the basic response to all beings that are capable of suffering. In the next chapter, we will focus more closely on the nature of compassion, but here we begin with suffering and its spiritual significance.

THE NATURE OF SUFFERING

What is suffering? Suffering includes the extremity of physical pain, as well as the emotional anguish and spiritual despair which every individual is bound to experience at some point in her life. It has been said that there is a significant difference between "pain" and "suffering," since the first is primarily "physical" while the latter is basically "mental." As Eliot Deutsch notes, "One has a pain or 'that is painful,' but 'I am suffering.' Where there is no ego there is no suffering—although

there might be pain."[8] And yet we express emotional suffering in physical terms when we say that we are *tortured* by guilt, or burning with
shame, or that our heart *aches* because of something that has happened
to us. Indeed, it would not be surprising if *every* form of suffering,
including those which are primarily "spiritual" or "emotional" had a
physical correlate in the body itself—fear is both physical and mental,
for example, and depression always has a somatic aspect. The upshot of
this is that it may be possible to understand the nature of suffering by
focusing on physical pain as its most direct and unmediated form.
Suffering is what hurts. In suffering, we experience the limits of self-
assertion, and the most extreme form of this is *physical* anguish, in
which the self is rendered passive and impotent by the torment that
ruins it as a subject. Herbert Fingarette puts this point succinctly when
he notes that "to suffer is to be compelled to endure, undergo, and
experience the humbled will, rather than to be able to impose one's
will."[9] This means that the experience of suffering is the opposite of
self-assertion, and it is filled with a sense of impotence and limitation.
Something like this is also the starting point for Levinas's own account
of what it is to suffer.

In the course of several books and numerous articles, Emmanuel
Levinas sketches the outlines of a phenomenology of suffering. Suffering is not always a central concern of his philosophy, but it is possible
to reconstruct his basic view of suffering by examining comments
drawn from several different texts. In *Time and the Other*, for example,
Levinas announces that he will focus his remarks on "the pain lightly
called physical," for "in it engagement in existence is without any
equivocation."[10] Once again, the point is that physical suffering is the
purest form of suffering since it completely overwhelms the *sovereignty* of the subject, for the pain can be so consuming it obliterates all
other matters of significance. Levinas notes that in *spiritual* suffering it
is still possible to preserve an attitude of dignity and distance from
whatever affects one, and in this respect one remains independent and
"free." Indeed, it can be argued that spiritual suffering is itself a kind of
"luxury" that can only exist for as long as we are not disturbed by
physical pain.

For Levinas, physical suffering involves the "irremissibility" of being and the absence of all refuge; in such pain we are backed up against
being with no possibility of escape, and for this reason it provides the
clearest, most unambiguous model for suffering in general. Significant
suffering corrodes all the structures of meaning that we project into the

world; it overwhelms our "virility"—or the effort to be masters of our own fate—until finally one is reduced to a state resembling helpless infancy: "Where suffering attains its purity, where there is no longer anything between us and it, the supreme responsibility of this extreme assumption turns into supreme irresponsibility, into infancy. Sobbing is this, and precisely through this it announces death. To die is to return to this state of irresponsibility, to be the infantile shaking of sobbing."[11] In her own account of torture, in *The Body in Pain*, Elaine Scarry confirms this when she points out that suffering and pain actively *destroy* language and all other meaningful projects, so that the subject reverts to "a state anterior to language, to the sounds and cries a human being makes before language is learned."[12] In this way, suffering is world-destroying. Indeed, to suffer greatly is to have one's world reduced to the content of one's pain.

Levinas notes a connection between suffering and death. In fact, he argues that the one announces the other:

> There is not only the feeling and the knowledge that suffering can end in death. Pain of itself includes it like a paroxysm, as if there were something about to be produced even more rending than suffering, as if despite the entire absence of a dimension of withdrawal that constitutes suffering, it still had some free space for an event, as if it must still get uneasy about something, as if we were on the verge of an event beyond what is revealed to the end in suffering. [13]

Extreme suffering involves complete passivity; in suffering we are subject to something which does not come from ourselves and which tends to undermine all the meaningful structures of subjectivity. In this respect, suffering is an anticipation of death since it is the encounter with something that cannot be avoided or held at arm's length. Both suffering and death involve the end of self-mastery, and in both, the contents of consciousness are destroyed. In his collection of essays, *At the Mind's Limits: Contemplations by a Survivor on Auschwitz and Its Realities,* Jean Améry, who was tortured by the Nazis, also seeks to articulate the strong connection between acute physical suffering and death. Speculating on the meaning of his own experience, he comments that

> Pain . . . is the most extreme intensification imaginable of our bodily being. But maybe it is even more, that is: death. No road that can be travelled by logic leads us to death, but perhaps the thought is permis-

sible that through pain a path of feeling and premonition can be paved
to it for us. In the end, we would be faced with the equation: Body =
Pain = Death, and in our case this could be reduced to the hypothesis
that torture, through which we are turned into body by the other, blots
out the contradiction of death and allows us to experience it personally.[14]

In extreme physical suffering, such as the torment that Améry describes, the individual becomes purely a body, and nothing else be-
sides. For as long as the pain continues, there is no possibility of reflection, and this violent reduction to physical being is the most intense
form of negation which seems to parallel the negation of death. Elaine
Scarry agrees: death and suffering are "the purest expressions of the
anti-human, of annihilation, of total aversiveness, though one is an
absence and the other a felt presence, one occurring in the cessation of
sentience, the other expressing itself in grotesque overload."[15]

Levinas elaborates his position on suffering in the essay "Transcendence and Evil," which is also a review of a book about Job, whose
sufferings are legendary.[16] In the Old Testament text, Job suffers emotional pain with the death of all his sons and daughters; he suffers the
physical pain of boils from his scalp to the soles of his feet; and he
suffers the moral anguish of being abandoned by God in spite of his
attempt to live a good life. Job suffers all of these pains at the hands of
Satan, who has persuaded God to let him test the extent of Job's devotion. In his anguish, he laments not only his own woes, but also the
suffering of other human beings, especially those who are innocent and
poor: "The poor, like herds of cattle/ wander across the plains,/ searching all day for food,/ picking up scraps for their children./ Naked,
without a refuge,/ they shiver in the bitter cold . . . /In the city the dying
groan/ and the wounded cry out for help;/ *but God sees nothing
wrong.*"[17]

Levinas focuses on several different aspects of the suffering or evil
that Job experiences. First, he argues that the basic quality of such evil
is *excess*. It is excessive in the sense that it cannot be grasped by the
subject who seeks to organize her world. As Levinas explains,

> Evil [*le mal*] is not an excess because suffering can be terrible, and go
> beyond the endurable. The break with the normal and the normative,
> with order, with synthesis, with the world, already constitutes its qual-
> itative essence. Suffering qua suffering is but a concrete and quasi-
> sensible manifestation of the non-integratable, the non-justifiable. The

quality of evil is this very non-integratability, if we can use such a term; this concrete quality is defined by this abstract notion. [18]

In this passage, Levinas seems to be saying that suffering is that which is excessive in itself; it is *always* "too much." As Cohen puts it, "little and great suffering are both suffering";[19] and so, the "too much" of pain is actually a part of its essence. More than this, suffering is not just "meaningless." It actively undermines the projection of meaning, and it brings about the undoing of the self as the one who would be subject of her own life.

Levinas points out that in the case of Job, the evil of suffering comes with a sense of persecution and individual torment. Suffering is never felt as something that just happens to me, but it is something that is done to me. Why me? we ask. What have I done to deserve this? And, why must *I* suffer in this way? In Levinas's words, "evil reaches me as though it sought me out; evil strikes me as though there were an aim behind the ill lot that pursues me, as though someone were set against me, as though there were malice, as though there were some one. Evil, of itself would be an 'aiming at me.'"[20] As we have seen, the great temptation is to interpret everything in terms of the meaningful projects of the self. Hence, suffering can be re-thought in terms of theodicy or some other meaningful goal: if I am suffering then perhaps I am being tested by God, or as his friends insist, Job must have done something to deserve it. In either case, I establish a relationship with the good that is beyond evil. It can be argued that from this religious perspective, "meaning then begins in the relationship of the soul with God, and begins with its awakening by evil. God does evil to me to tear me out of the world, as unique and ex-ceptional—as a soul."[21] For without suffering, it seems that I would never know what is good.

In this way, the discovery of evil—or the experience of suffering—involves the realization of the ethical as the ground of our being. Through his own suffering, Job becomes aware of the sufferings of others and our obligations to them. The existence of suffering illuminates the possibility of the good. Levinas warns us, however: "Is this horror of evil in which, paradoxically, it is given, the Good? There can here be no question of a passage from Evil to the Good through the attraction of contraries; that would make but one more theodicy."[22] As we suggested earlier, the problem of suffering seems to inaugurate much of philosophy and religion, and it clearly inspires the development of Stoicism and Epicureanism, Christianity, Buddhism, and Judaism to name but some among many. Not, "How did the world get here?" but "Why is there suffering?" is the first provocation to thought. But once again, the great temptation of theodicy is to disregard suffering or even to justify it as an expression of God's will or the progress of History.

So far, then, we have isolated at least four different aspects of Levinas's own philosophy of suffering which are clearly mapped out in his writings. First, suffering involves the impossibility of escape, or what he calls the "irremissibility" of being. In suffering I am backed up against the world, and I can do nothing. Second, suffering is the end of all mastery and "virility," and in this sense, suffering involves the intimation of death. Third, suffering is excessive: it is the non-integratable and the failure of self-control. All of these aspects point toward the way in which suffering involves radical passivity. For Levinas, suffering is not the denial of freedom, or the frustration of any desires that I may have. As he comments in this difficult passage, it is the complete overwhelming of the self:

> Suffering is a pure undergoing. It is not a matter of a passivity which would degrade man by striking a blow against his freedom. Pain would limit such freedom to the point of compromising self-consciousness, permitting man the identity of the thing only in the passivity of the submission. The evil which rends the humanity of the suffering person overwhelms his humanity otherwise than non-freedom overwhelms it: violently and cruelly, more irremissibly than the negation which dominates or paralyzes the act in non-freedom . . . The evil of pain, the harm itself, is the explosion and most profound articulation of absurdity.[23]

Finally, the fourth point that Levinas makes is that suffering is experienced as something that is done to me—whether in the course of nature or at the hands of other people, I experience myself as a victim, and not as the agent of my own existence. In this respect, suffering becomes the origin of meaning and justification, for it evokes the response of theodicy and its equivalents—"there must be a good reason why it happened," or "it was meant to be," etc. Suffering inspires the reassertion of meaning in the face of its destruction.

Levinas's discussion of suffering is compelling and to some extent his account is confirmed by Scarry and Améry, who write from very different standpoints. But to what extent can one ever speak about suffering in general? In the end, suffering is just whatever hurts. And beyond this, all suffering, whether spiritual, emotional, or physical, involves the unsettling or destruction of my world; it isolates me, making me feel powerless and a victim.

THE MEANING OF SUFFERING

The second question is, Can suffering ever be meaningful? As we have already noted, some philosophers, including Nietzsche, exhort the value of suffering because it promotes "character." In *Beyond Good and Evil*, Nietzsche claims that, "profound suffering makes noble";[24] in *The Gay Science*, he says that, "only great pain is the ultimate liberator of the spirit";[25] and in *Thus Spoke Zarathustra*, he describes the *sickness* of the modern world in trying to eliminate all pain: "'We have invented happiness,' say the last men, and they blink."[26] Of course, it may well be the case that some kind of struggle is necessary for living a flourishing life, and the possibility of a successful struggle also comes with the possibility of failure and the suffering that failure entails. But we are more concerned with the most extreme forms of suffering that completely destroy the well-being of people without any possibility of redemption in the future. For example, the suffering of those who are mentally handicapped, who cannot understand their suffering or communicate it to others.[27] How could such pointless, unreflective pain finally be recuperated into the context of a meaningful life? Or following Ivan's ruminations in *The Brothers Karamazov*, how can we reconcile the suffering and the murder of children with the goodness of creation? How could such things ever be "for the best"?

In his essay, "Useless Suffering," Levinas focuses on the mountain of suffering that belongs to the twentieth century. Such excessive suffering—the torture and destruction of millions of innocent people—the elderly, children, even babies—calls into question the traditional conception of God as supremely powerful and supremely good, and appears to undermine "theodicy" as a lie. And now, when some people even deny that the Holocaust ever happened, the suffering of those who endured the Holocaust has apparently become more pointless than ever. Levinas explains: "This would be pain in its undiluted malignity, suffering for nothing. It renders impossible and odious every proposal and every thought which would explain it by the sins of those who have suffered or are dead."[28] This leads him to argue that theodicy as the justification of the other person's pain, is "certainly the source of all immorality."[29] In the case of the Holocaust, it was the bystanders, and not just the perpetrators, who allowed this great evil to happen, using rationalization and justification which implied that the victims deserved their fate. In this regard, theodicy is not a good thing, but actually an evil and a temptation insofar as it turns us away from the reality of someone else's suffering by framing it within the context of a larger metaphysical order.

But Levinas never says that *all* suffering is meaningless. As we have already noted, he claims that sometimes suffering can become meaningful insofar as it reveals the ethical dimension of human experience. For even though the suffering of the other cannot be made meaningful from my perspective, my own suffering can have meaning when it is suffering in response to the suffering of another person:

> In this perspective a radical difference develops between *suffering in the other*, which for *me* is unpardonable and solicits me and calls me, and suffering *in me*, my own adventure of suffering, whose constitutional or congenital uselessness can take on a meaning, the only meaning to which suffering is susceptible, in becoming a suffering for the suffering—be it inexorable—of someone else. [30]

This is the "inter-human" region of being that exists insofar as I acknowledge the suffering of the other and his claims upon me. And according to Levinas:

> It is this attention to the Other which, across the cruelties of our century—despite these cruelties, because of these cruelties—can be affirmed as the very bond of human subjectivity, even to the point of being raised to a supreme ethical principle—the only one which it is not possible to contest—a principle which can go so far as to command the hopes and practical discipline of vast human groups. [31]

We are summoned to responsibility by the face of the other that commands our obedience *now*.

At one point in his essay, "Useless Suffering," Levinas elaborates his position on the possibility of *useful* suffering, in terms of *compassion*, which other thinkers, including Schopenhauer, Rousseau, Nussbaum, and a long line of Buddhist writers, have also viewed as the key to morality. According to Martha Nussbaum, compassion is fundamental and it must be cultivated because it is the basic social emotion. [32] Levinas puts it this way: "Must not humanity now, in a faith more difficult than ever, in a faith without theodicy, continue Sacred History;

a history which now demands even more of the resources of the *self* in each one, and appeals to its suffering inspired by the suffering of the other person, to its compassion which is a non-useless suffering (or love), which is no longer suffering 'for nothing,' and which straight-away has a meaning?"³³ Here, Levinas seems to be claiming that my own suffering becomes meaningful when it is suffering which is for the other person. But how exactly does this work? One possibility is that by cultivating an awareness of the suffering of others, and by using my moral imagination to identify with their plight, I can develop my natural compassion, and in this way I may become more responsive to the needs of other people. Also, by facing up to my *own* suffering—rather than ignoring it—I can learn to be more aware of the suffering of others, and in this way I will be more available to help them. Something like this would be the Buddhist position on suffering which we will consider in the next chapter. But is this what Levinas has in mind in the passage quoted above, when he talks about "compassion"?

It is tempting to identify Levinas with an appeal to universal love, but for Levinas we are obligated to the other regardless of how we feel about it. And while I may feel compassion, I may just as easily feel *resentment* because I am responsible for the other person even though I never asked to be! I am a "victim" and a "hostage," but not because of anything that I have done or could have anticipated: "Obsessed with responsibilities, which do not result from decisions taken by a 'freely contemplating' subject, consequently accused of what it never willed or decreed, accused of what it did not do, subjectivity is thrown back on itself—in itself—by a persecuting accusation."³⁴ The moral anguish that Levinas describes in this passage (and in many others) derives from the "infinite" burden of responsibility that I am made aware of in the face of the other person: the homeless person, the wayward companion, the refugee. I feel that I am bound to help him even if I know that he would never help me. And the recognition of this responsibility in no way depends upon "melting compassion" or "love." For Levinas, ethics is not about flourishing, and it is more about being chosen than choosing. It is traumatic to be called to such infinite responsibility, but as far as he is concerned, this is the *only* meaningful suffering, which is *suffering for the suffering of the other*.

In sketching the ethical relationship, Levinas describes a powerful drama of anguish and subjection. But what is most important is not the sympathetic contagion of the other's distress; it is the *claim* that the other makes upon me, regardless of who he is, and regardless of how I feel about it. In Levinas's account, the other is remote and unattainable. I need not recognize the possibility of my own suffering when I look at him. We have nothing in common (from the ethical point of view); I cannot expect reciprocity from him, and what links us is, precisely, difference. In this respect, we must conclude that for Levinas true compassion or empathy is impossible and also irrelevant since my responsibility cannot wait for me to feel the suffering of the other person.

The problem with this view is that it fails to recognize that what is properly meaningful is not suffering itself but our *response* to suffering. For example, if my suffering leads me to commit suicide then in what sense can it be considered meaningful? And if my awareness of the suffering of another becomes so overwhelming it paralyzes action, does it really have a meaning or a point? Suffering is neither "meaningful" nor "meaningless" in itself. What determines the significance of suffering is the *response* of the one who suffers. This could be the original victim—someone like Elie Wiesel who lost his family in the Holocaust, but who sought to live a life devoted to justice, *or* it could be the spectator who suffers in sorrow when she contemplates these events and who feels compelled to respond. In this respect, my suffering, the suffering of the other, and my suffering *for* the suffering of the other all remain quite "open" in terms of their ultimate meaning.

RESPONSES TO SUFFERING

Finally, then, the third question asks what the proper response to suffering should be. Here, we can consider three possibilities: indifference, self-overcoming, and compassion, which are associated with Stoicism, Nietzsche's philosophy, and Buddhism respectively. Stoicism appears to cultivate indifference to suffering. According to the Stoics, the goal of human existence is to live in accordance with nature, Providence, or Zeus (the various names for the divine reason of the cosmos itself). Since our own reason is an offshoot of reason in the universe at large— "or a small fragment of that which is perfect," we should live in accordance with human virtue or natural law.[35] For the Stoics, to be moral was everything, and this meant we should seek good things, avoid bad things, and be indifferent to those things that are indifferent, which includes everything except virtue itself. We may decide to pursue things which are indifferent, strictly speaking, but we must not forget that such "preferred indifferents"—including health or power—are at best an indirect means of pursuing virtue.

One of the reasons for the great popularity of Stoicism in the ancient world was because it offered people a philosophy they could live by; as Pierre Hadot remarks, like other ancient schools of philosophy, it was primarily *formative* rather than *informative* in character. For one thing, the writings of the Stoic philosophers contained numerous spiritual exercises and even thought experiments that could move the individual beyond the level of the ordinary self to "thinking and acting in union with universal reason."[36] We should keep in mind that whatever happens is a part of the ultimate necessity of the world, and we should train ourselves to accept the decrees of Providence. As Epictetus puts it, "Do not seek to have events happen as you want them to, but instead want them to happen as they do happen, and your life will go well."[37] And Marcus Aurelius advises, "Do not be aggrieved, then, if things are not always to your liking. As long as they are in accord with nature, be glad of them, and do not to make difficulties."[38]

Such passages emphasize the goodness of the world. As the Stoics never ceased to insist, one should not complain about what happens or be upset about the shortness of life or reverses of fortune, because the universe is inherently moral in nature and whatever happens is in accordance with divine reason. Hence the Stoic sage is someone who remains open to whatever happens and possesses equanimity in the face of disaster or death. The fact is, we can't control what happens in the world; we can't control our bodies, our possessions, our reputations, or anything except our own inner life. As Epictetus says at the very beginning of his *Handbook*, "Some things are up to us and some things are not up to us. Our opinions are up to us, and our impulses, desires, aversions—in short, whatever is our own doing."[39] And in section 2,

> So detach your aversion from everything not up to us, and transfer it to what is against nature among the things that are up to us. And for the time being eliminate desire completely, since if you desire something that is not up to us, you are bound to be unfortunate, and at the same time none of the things that are up to us, which it would be good to desire, will be available to you. Make use only of impulse and its contrary, rejection, though with reservation, lightly, and without straining.[40]

In this way, the Stoics emphasize how it is possible to live within the inner citadel of personal freedom—and this is the core aspect of our being which is both sovereign and separate from everything else.

The Stoics emphasize that our health and material well-being are *not* under our control. We must try to live a good life, but in the end, we may get sick, we may find ourselves under the rule of a cruel master, or we may lose our fortune. So how are we to respond to such events? For the Stoics, wealth, health, and reputation are ultimately indifferent since they can lead to good or evil. Virtue is the only thing that we should actively pursue, since virtue is the only thing that is good without qualification. And so we should learn to accept suffering and misfortune as things that are ultimately indifferent to our own well-being. For example, "Illness interferes with the body, not with one's faculty of choice, unless that faculty of choice wishes it to. Lameness interferes with the limb, not with one's faculty of choice. Say this at each thing that happens to you, since you will find that it interferes with something else, not with you."[41] This suggests that the self is always beyond whatever happens to the body. We can always choose how to respond to things, and the Stoics imply that we can train ourselves to choose in the right way. If we are afraid of losing someone, for example, we may anticipate her death so that we will not be overcome by grief when she dies: "if you kiss your child or your wife, say that you are kissing a human being; for when it dies you will not be upset."[42]

In this way, Stoicism preaches indifference to suffering in the final analysis. And this implies that the true Stoic will not rail against his unjust treatment at the hands of others—or at the hands of the cosmos itself—because whatever happens is in accordance with divine law, and as good servants we should desire that things will happen exactly as they do. One further passage from Epictetus captures this attitude through the metaphor of drama: "Remember that you are an actor in a play, which is as the playwright wants it to be: short if he wants it short, long if he wants it long. If he wants you to play a beggar, play even this part skilfully, or a cripple, or a public official, or a private citizen. What is yours is to play the assigned part well. But to choose it belongs to someone else."[43]

In response to this, I think it has to be said that Stoicism is unrealistic. To what extent can we really *choose* how we respond to suffering? Certainly, there are some things that we can choose—to control our grief or to express it—but at a certain point, the self, which is supposedly independent and self-contained—may be completely swept away by the suffering it undergoes. Marcus Aurelius talks about pain and suffering as things that are separate from us. He writes:

> Pain must be an evil either to the body—in which case let the body speak for itself—or if not, to the soul. But the soul can always refuse to consider it an evil, and so keep its skies unclouded and its calm unruffled. For there is no decision, no impulse, no movement of approach or recoil, but must proceed from within the self; and into this self no evil can force its way.[44]

But the fact is, we *can't* simply choose our responses to whatever happens, for the self is not a separate, self-contained principle. The self belongs to the world, and it is formed by its relationships with others, as well as its connection to the material reality that the body is composed of. Hence, the self can become sick, sleep-deprived, and physically ruined. There are stories of Epictetus and other Stoics remaining indifferent to overwhelming pain in the course of torture, but this seems questionable. The infliction of massive suffering only unravels or destroys the self and returns it to a purely animal functioning. Also, saying we can *choose* how to respond to the loss of a loved one is unrealistic because our sense of who we are is completely bound up with those we love. The alternative would be to *avoid* loving relationships altogether, because they undermine our self-mastery.

The Stoics claim that cosmology has an ethical dimension—we must embrace whatever happens because it belongs to the divine order of the universe itself. But why should I simply accept the death of a loved one or my own terminal disease? Is it because I can't do anything else about it and so this is just being realistic? Or is it that by accepting these things I am reasserting my own power by choosing what has already happened? But this seems like self-deception. I would retain more power by choosing to affirm or reject events according to my own judgment. Certainly, I would never say that the Holocaust was a wise decision on the part of the cosmos itself. In the end, Stoicism is not an appropriate response to suffering because it is psychologically unrealistic, and it implies a thoughtless theodicy that is even more difficult to relate to today. More than this, however, we might wonder whether we *should* try to cultivate an attitude of indifference to suffering, even if we could, for this implies an avoidance of the problem rather than coming to terms with it in a more authentic way.

In the ancient world, suffering was ubiquitous and formed an inevitable part of life. Suffering seemed to be unavoidable. In the modern world, however, the growth of humanitarianism and prosperity in the West has led to the belief that suffering is something that *can* be overcome. For example, utilitarianism prospered in the nineteenth century as a philosophy that sought to increase the net level of happiness by reducing pain and suffering and promoting whatever led to a more comfortable existence. Now, for the first time, we have come to think of suffering as something that we are responsible for, not an inevitable feature of existence, but something to be overcome through better medicine, better food, and more just political arrangements.

In complete opposition to this, Nietzsche has nothing but scorn for the optimistic vision of human progress that seeks to end all suffering and pain. In *Thus Spoke Zarathustra*, he is contemptuous of the "last man" who may be regarded as the final outcome of this rational progress and the fulfilment of the humanistic ideal: "The Earth has become small, and on it hops the last man, who makes everything small. He is as ineradicable as the flea beetle; the last man lives longest. We have invented happiness, say the last men, and they blink."[45] In response to this *false* ideal, Nietzsche cultivates the goal of the *overman,* an individual who embodies the continual self-overcoming of life, and he praises the overman as the complete justification of human existence. But Nietzsche also argues that only great suffering inspires self-overcoming, and hence, suffering is not a "problem" to be solved since it inspires self-enhancement. In *Beyond Good and Evil*, he is insistent:

> You want, if possible—and there is no more insane "if possible"—to *abolish suffering*. And we? It really seems that *we* would rather have it higher and worse than ever. Well-being as you understand it—that is no goal, that seems to us an end, a state that soon makes men ridiculous and contemptible—that makes his destruction *desirable*. The discipline of suffering, of *great* suffering—do you not know that only *this* discipline has created all enhancements of man so far? That tension of the soul in unhappiness which cultivates its strength, its shudders face-to-face with great ruin, its inventiveness and courage in enduring, persevering, interpreting, and exploiting suffering, and whatever has been granted to it of profundity, secret, mask, spirit, cunning, and greatness—was it not granted to it through suffering, through the discipline of great suffering?[46]

This is an important passage because it encapsulates a typical attitude toward suffering which says that suffering is a good thing insofar as it can make us stronger and inspires self-overcoming. In his writings, Nietzsche has great contempt for pity and he even thinks of it as the greatest danger, because it leads us to abandon our own authentic path for the sake of others—and he thinks this can only lead to the reduction of human life. By contrast, he urges us to avoid pity and become hard: "For all creators are hard. And it must seem blessedness to you to impress your hand on millennia as on wax . . . This new tablet, O my brothers, I place over you: become hard!"[47]

In the light of the Holocaust and other catastrophes of recent times, the injunction to become hard is profoundly problematic.[48] Becoming hard is actually the least spiritual path, for it requires the destruction of spirituality, which is associated with openness to the other and to the world itself. When we idealize our own self-sufficiency and glorify our ability to control pain as a sign of our strength and self-control, it becomes that much easier to inflict pain and suffering on others. "How strong are you?" quickly becomes "How much pain can you bear?" Once we become hard, we are capable of inflicting great suffering on others without really being affected by it. In the end, the final goal is to become so hard that all sensitivity to pain and suffering has been overcome. But just as in Stoicism, this leads to separation and isolation from the rest of the world. It is a kind of spiritual death that closes us off from an authentic encounter with others.

Much of recent human history has been a catalogue of cruelties practiced, or condoned, by those who have been taught to be hard and unflinching in their devotion to the cause. In cruelty, we exult in other people's suffering—we even say that it serves them right! Cruelty is made possible by the cancellation of the basic conditions for compassion that include openness and availability to the other. Cruelty and compassion are in this respect opposites, and the virtue of compassion must be cultivated if only to avoid the horrendous cruelties that have characterized much of human history up to this point.

Emmanuel Levinas claims that suffering can only be validated when it is suffering for the other. At the same time, it must be noted that compassion is not a central part of his ethical framework, and he comments, "for me the suffering of compassion, suffering because the other suffers, is only one aspect of a relationship that is much more complex and much more complete at the same time: that of responsibility for the other."[49] Levinas's ethics is severe, and the traumatic relation to the other person seems to rely entirely on duty rather than love. Again, he writes,

I am in reality responsible for the other even when he or she commits crimes, even when others commit crimes. This is for me the essence of the Jewish conscience. But I also think that it is the essence of the human conscience. All men are responsible for one another, and "I more than anyone else." One of the most important things for me is that asymmetry and that formula: All men are responsible for each other and I more than anyone else. [50]

Against this view of compassion, which emphasizes guilt and the suffering of self-laceration, we may now consider another version of compassion which follows the Buddhist model. This involves feeling empathy for the other's distress, and it presupposes recognition of the common humanity that we all share. And this is an attitude that we can learn to cultivate, for in the end we can only be moved by the other person because she suffers like we do, and because we all share a common fate. In the next chapter, we shall look at compassion, primarily from the perspective of Buddhist and Christian philosophy, which justify compassion as the most authentic response to suffering.

Chapter Two

Compassion

According to the Dalai Lama, compassion is the supreme emotion, and together with love it is the source of all spiritual qualities, "including forgiveness, tolerance, and all the virtues."[1] Buddhists, such as the Dalai Lama, affirm compassion both as a primary virtue and as a form of wisdom, and they regard the most enlightened being as the one who is most compassionate. Christianity also celebrates compassion, which can be viewed as a fundamental aspect of Christian love, or *agape*. The parable of the Good Samaritan epitomizes Christian compassion, and it shows that such caring is to be valued as an expression of inner strength. By contrast, *philosophers* tend to be more critical of compassion, and they are uncomfortable with related ideas such as pity, sympathy, and sometimes, even love. What is the reason for such a fundamental difference between religion and philosophy on this point? And *can* philosophy help us to understand the nature of compassion in its spiritual context? This chapter looks at the place of compassion in the emergence of our spiritual life, for in responding to the other, we put aside our own selfish projects and enter into a greater reality. Without this our spiritual life would be stillborn.

We begin with the Buddhist teaching on compassion and then compare it to the Christian point of view. For even though Christianity and Buddhism have different metaphysical perspectives, they remain close insofar as both of them affirm the necessity of compassion. But what exactly does compassion involve? Clearly, the meaning of compassion depends upon the experience of the one who feels compassion as well as the one who receives it. But it also requires an account that distinguishes compassion from related ideas such as pity, empathy, and love. The *value* of compassion must be considered, and we can look at philosophical challenges to compassion and related ideas, such as pity, which have been raised by Nietzsche, Kant, and the Stoic philosophers. The question here is whether philosophy shows the limitations of compassion, or if we can we use philosophy to enhance our understanding of what compassion is. Finally, since compassion is the primary spiritual response, and the only adequate response to suffering, we must ask in what ways we can *cultivate* compassion to make it a more significant part of our lives.

BUDDHIST AND CHRISTIAN VIEWS OF COMPASSION

In Buddhist teaching there are four sublime states that we should strive to cultivate, especially through the practice of meditation. These are loving-kindness (*metta*), sympathetic joy (*mudita*), equanimity (*upekkha*), and compassion (*karuna*). Of all of these, however, compassion is considered the most important, and for many Buddhists it is the fundamental virtue and the key to ethics itself. As the Dalai Lama notes, "Ethically wholesome actions arise naturally in the context of compassion."[2] The Buddha himself is known as the compassionate one because he decided to communicate his teaching to others before he departed from this world. And the *bodhisattva*, the Buddhist saint who has achieved enlightenment, refuses to enter nirvana until all other sentient beings have been released from their suffering. In the *Prajnaparamita Sutra*, such an ideal is described in more detail:

> Doers of what is hard are the bodhisattvas, the great beings who have set out to win supreme enlightenment. They do not wish to attain their own private nirvana. On the contrary. They have surveyed the highly painful world of being, and yet, desirous to win supreme enlightenment, they do not tremble at birth and death. They have set out for the benefit of the world, for the ease of the world, out of pity for the world. They have resolved "We will become a shelter for the world, a refuge for the world, the world's place of rest, the final relief of the world, islands of the world, lights of the world, leaders of the world, the world's means of salvation."[3]

On the face of it, this is a magnificent impulse which follows from true greatness of soul. But the bodhisattva is not a "heroic" individual since he has lost the sense of being a separate person whose interests could be in opposition to others. He is inspired by the most complete and unconditional compassion which responds to all of the suffering in the world, and the enlightenment and well-being of others is his only concern.

In Buddhism, compassion *begins* with the feeling of sadness and sorrow for the misfortunes of others, which we might think of as empathy or pity. But in its fullest form, compassion can be viewed as a kind of wisdom which reflects our attunement to the underlying reality of the world. Most of us are fixated on our own lives and the private joys and miseries that characterize our everyday existence. But at the same time, there are usually people that we care about, and their happiness and disappointment affect us, so that our own well-being is completely bound up with theirs. If we could extend this even further, and feel the same kind of sympathy or compassion for strangers—or for other sentient creatures, such as cows, chickens, and even smaller animals—then we might eventually identify with all beings and experience universal compassion. Certainly, the more we care about others and become mindful of their suffering, the more we soften our sense of self, and the idea that each of us is just a separate self-contained existence becomes harder to accept. As the Dalai Lama explains:

> For most of us, when we confront the sight of suffering—for example, a child crying, a man in agony, people dying of starvation—our immediate visceral reaction is sympathy. Often we feel as if we ourselves are undergoing this suffering. There is a certain spontaneity and directness in our natural reaction. It touches us profoundly as human beings. Such a reaction may seem inexplicable from a strictly rational point of view, but it indicates a profound interconnectedness among all living beings. [4]

We could also point out that almost everything in our lives has been provided for by others, from the buildings that we live and work in, to the clothes that we wear, the roads we travel on, and the food that we eat—and this testifies to the reality of *interdependence* as the basic human condition.

For Buddhists, then, the extension of empathy is also the experience of true wisdom because the world *is* completely interconnected and interdependent; there are no separate self-contained beings that always remain the same, and the ultimate reality—as opposed to the everyday perspective of people and things—has no fundamental essence: in fact it is defined by "emptiness" (*sunyatta*), or the *absence* of fixed, substantial forms that would ensure that each thing would be separate from everything else. In *Buddhism without Beliefs*, Stephen Batchelor insists upon the importance of meditation to incorporate these truths into the deepest level of our experience. For as he notes, this is more than just a matter of intellectual understanding:

> Insight into emptiness and compassion for the world are two sides of the same coin. To experience ourselves and the world as interactive processes rather than aggregates of discrete things undermines both habitual ways of perceiving the world as well as habitual feelings about it. Meditative discipline is vital to Dharma practice precisely because it leads us beyond the realm of ideas to that of felt experience. Understanding the philosophy of emptiness is not enough. The ideas need to be translated through meditation into the wordless language of feeling in order to loosen those emotional knots that keep us locked in a spasm of self-preoccupation. As we are released into the opening left by the absence of self-centred craving, we experience the vulnerability of exposure to the anguish and suffering of the world.[5]

From this point of view, compassion really is the fundamental spiritual quality that puts us in touch with ultimate reality and meaning. It is both an ethical and an ontological key which illuminates the way the world is, and it allows us to experience spiritual enlightenment.

Agape, which is Christian love or charity, is very closely related to Buddhist compassion (or *karuna*). For one thing, *agape*, in distinction to friendship or romantic love, is an "impersonal" or "disinterested" kind of love in which we care about other people not because we have strong personal feelings for them but just because they are human beings, God's creatures, and therefore worthy of love. For Thomas Aquinas, compassion is an effect of charity, which is defined as the friendship of humans for God, and he claims that our friendship with God inspires us to love everything that He has created. Aquinas points out that when we love someone, we typically love that person's children because they are in a sense an extension of the person that we care about. Likewise, he says that in loving God, we are bound to love all of God's children, and since He is the father of us all we should delight in his creation. But such a power of love does not originate from the individual's own will, for on the face of it, it would be difficult, if not impossible to love those that we don't have a personal connection with, let alone to love our enemies. According to Aquinas, the explanation for this must be that the Holy Spirit infuses the act of love by moving a person's will so that he or she is finally inclined to love others:

> A thing's quantity depends on its proper cause, because a more univer-
> sal cause produces a greater effect. Now charity, as stated above, since
> it altogether transcends human nature, does not depend on any natural
> virtue, but solely on the grace of the Holy Spirit who infuses it. Accord-
> ingly its quantity does not depend on the quality of the nature or on the
> capacity of its natural virtue, but exclusively on the will of the Holy
> Spirit who distributes his gifts as he pleases. As St. Paul says, *To each
> of us is given grace according to the measure of the giving of Christ.*[6]

Such a universal love is remarkable, and even irrational, but it does happen, and when it happens it fills the individual with a strong sense of peace, regardless of the response she receives from others. Skeptics may say that the explanation of the Holy Spirit is just another way of emphasizing the "impossible" character of such love which seems to come from outside us, since we are painfully aware of our own limitations. But it must also be noted that Christian love or the love of one's neighbor, broadly conceived, is characterized by non-attachment—it is not based on personal desire for the other person—who may be a complete stranger—and in this respect it is similar to Buddhist compassion.

Later, in the *Summa Theologiae*, Aquinas discusses *misericordia* (or mercy), which seems to be a similar idea to what we would call compassion.[7] Aquinas begins by quoting St. Augustine, who says that "mercy [*misericordia*] is heartfelt compassion for another's misery, a compassion which drives us to do what we can to help him."[8] He goes on to point out that the word *misericordia* comes from *miserum cor*, or one's heart being sad at the sight of another's distress. Now of course, there are significant differences between Aquinas's account of *misericordia* and the Buddhist concept of *karuna*, but once we leave aside the *metaphysical* context of each perspective, including beliefs about God and personal immortality, we find that there are broad similarities in the way that compassion is conceived. First, within the human community, at least, Christian compassion is potentially unlimited in scope: it is certainly not limited to the righteous, or to those who "deserve" compassion, and in this respect it follows the example of Christ's ministry on earth. As Aquinas points out, "It is in this sense that we have mercy on sinners and pity them. . . . And in Matthew we read that when Jesus saw the crowds he had compassion on them, because they were harassed and helpless, like sheep without a shepherd."[9] Second, Aquinas emphasizes the ways in which compassion may be cultivated and developed through imaginative identification with those who are unhappy: "and so sadness over another's misfortune is measured by the extent to which we see another's misfortune as our own."[10] Here, Aquinas emphasizes that compassion is a virtue—not just a feeling—which can be cultivated or regulated by right reason. Not to feel compassion for another's misfortune would be a failing, and this implies that we must have some control over this response. Finally, Aquinas goes so far as to say that compassion is the greatest virtue since it is the most godlike of all the virtues, "for it involves the giving from one's abundance to others, and, what is more, relieving their needs, a function especially belonging to a superior. This is why we say that mercy is something proper to God, and that it is here, above all, that he shows his almighty power."[11] Hence, in regard to other people, compassion is the greatest virtue, although Aquinas asserts that charity is an even greater virtue since it unites us with God.

In the *Summa*, Aquinas also argues that the highest level of charity involves a kind of self-abandonment: "When a man applies himself chiefly to the work of cleaving to God and enjoying him, which is characteristic of the perfect who long to depart and to be with Christ."[12] Significantly, the Latin here is *cupiunt dissolve et esse cum Christe*—so if we think of compassion as a manifestation of charity, then the goal of compassion must also involve self-dissolution or self-abandonment in the fullness of absolute being. These three points—the unlimited scope of compassion—at least within the human community—or the fact that compassion does not depend upon desert; the stress on cultivating compassion as a virtue; and the greatness of compassion, which inspires us with the desire to lose ourselves to become part of a higher reality—are significant features of compassion in both the Buddhist and the Christian traditions. In this respect, both versions of compassion may derive from a common intuition concerning its essential truth.

Immediately after his enlightenment, the Buddha preaches the Fire Sermon, in which he proclaims that attachment and desire are the root cause of all suffering. He never advocates indifference or detachment from life, but instead he urges us to care for others in a non-attached way, without desire or personal interests clouding the issue. Similarly, in the New Testament, Jesus tells the parable of the Good Samaritan, in which the compassion and love shown by the Good Samaritan is not based on friendship or any kind of personal desire. Jesus says we should love our neighbor, and he uses this parable to show the meaning of Christian love or *agape* as a disinterested form of caring:

> A man was going down from Jerusalem to Jericho, and he fell among robbers, who stripped him and beat him, and departed, leaving him half dead. Now by chance a priest was going down that road; and when he saw him he passed by on the other side. So likewise a Levite, when he came to the place and saw him, passed by on the other side. But a Samaritan, as he journeyed, came to where he was; and when he saw him, he had compassion, and went to him and bound up his wounds, pouring on oil and wine; then he set him on his own beast and brought him to an inn, and took care of him. And the next day he took out two denarii and gave them to the innkeeper, saying, "Take care of him; and whatever more you spend, I will repay you when I come back." [13]

The story is really all about the compassionate response of the Samaritan who cared about the suffering of another man and wanted to help him, even though he had never met him before. In context, it is not clear what the Samaritan's duties were, and certainly, nobody expected him to help. The Samaritan had nothing to gain by helping the man, who had lost everything, and there is no suggestion that he acted for the sake of heavenly rewards. In this case, such disinterested caring arises from the inability to ignore another's suffering, and so it is really the essence of compassion itself. Indeed, such a response would be valued by most religious traditions as a significant spiritual virtue.

So far we have emphasized the similarity between Christian love and Buddhist compassion. But the two are not entirely identical, and certainly the commandment to "love thy neighbor" is more difficult than the commandment which urges us to be compassionate. It is probably easier to care for somebody who is suffering or unhappy because we typically respond to another's vulnerability, and even if we don't like someone, if he becomes sick or suffers a personal tragedy, we are bound to feel sympathy for him. It is much harder to *love* someone who is arrogant and oblivious of the needs of other people, and this suggests that compassion is the basis of our original connection to others. But all agapic love includes compassion; in fact, it begins with compassion as the primary way in which we come to identify with others and take their well-being seriously. Christians and Buddhists may have very different beliefs. Christians believe in God as the Supreme Being, and they believe in the immortality of the soul, whereas Buddhists question both of these things. But in spite of these differences, both Christians and Buddhists affirm compassion as a fundamental good.

Now there is some conflict between Buddhism and Christianity concerning the proper limits to compassion. Buddhists tend to believe that compassion should be unlimited and universal in scope, and they affirm that it must include all sentient beings, including animals who suffer terribly in factory farms, in hunting, and in the course of medical research. Christianity tends to limit compassion to human beings because of the belief that animals lack rational souls, and yet it affirms that we should feel love and compassion for all humans, including those "sinners" who have committed crimes and hurt other people. By contrast, there is another *philosophical* tradition on compassion, which includes Aristotle, Rousseau, and more recently, Martha Nussbaum. These thinkers assert that compassion should be discriminating, and for various reasons, they argue that it would be a mistake, or even morally wrong, to feel compassion for a vicious human being or even for an animal. According to this philosophical perspective, such people (or creatures) do not deserve compassion because they have forfeited the right to be cared for (or they never had it in the first place). But by tying compassion to rational judgment, these thinkers miss the respect in which compassion is the most basic condition of *generosity* which refuses to calculate or judge. We will focus on generosity in the next chapter, but now we must refine the meaning of *compassion*.

THE MEANING OF COMPASSION

So what exactly is compassion, and what is its spiritual significance? As we saw in the previous chapter, suffering isolates me, and the pain or the grief that I experience takes me out of the everyday world that I usually lose myself in. I am pinned down by my suffering, and no one can share my pain because suffering is a private event which cannot be exchanged with others. Compassion is one of the primary responses to suffering, and it involves openness to the other person and the acknowledgement of her pain. The fact is that when we suffer, we feel alienated and isolated from other people, but the compassion of another person, even if it is only given in a kind look, helps to restore us to the human community, and we feel better about ourselves if we know that someone cares about our well-being. In his holocaust memoir, Primo Levi describes how in Auschwitz the compassionate concern of a stranger helped to keep him alive by restoring a sense of his own humanity. Lorenzo did not have much to give him, but just by showing concern and caring, he reminded Levi that he was still a human being. As Levi notes, "I believe that it was really due to Lorenzo that I am alive today, and not so much for his material aid, as for his having constantly reminded me by his presence, by his natural and plain manner of being good, that there still existed a just world outside our own, something and someone still pure and whole, not corrupt. . . . Thanks to Lorenzo, I managed not to forget that I myself was a man."[14] Elaine Scarry also comments that even in extreme physical suffering, "an act of human contact and concern, whether occurring here or in private contexts of sympathy, provides the hurt person with worldly self-extension . . . By holding that world in place, or by giving the pain a place in the world, sympathy lessens the power of sickness and pain, counteracts the force with which a person in great pain or sickness can be swallowed alive by the body."[15] In this way, sympathy or compassion works to overcome the isolation that suffering imposes. Likewise, the one who feels compassion cannot easily separate her own well-being from the well-being of others, for the suffering of others makes her suffer too. And by refusing to accept that someone else's suffering could ever be a matter of indifference, we come to identify our own well-being with the well-being of everyone else.

Many writers, including Rousseau and Schopenhauer, have pointed out that compassion inspires a strong sense of our own vulnerability. Someone else has suffered a terrible misfortune, and the compassionate response involves the awareness that this could just as easily have been me. Similarly, Aristotle claims that dramatic tragedy evokes the feelings of fear and pity; we not only feel badly for Oedipus or the other tragic heroes who have to undergo much suffering, but we also fear for ourselves: there but for the grace of God go I, and what separates me from the afflicted person is nothing that cannot be removed by a change in circumstances. In this way, compassion seems to strip away all the surface distinctions between people and leaves us with a strong sense of our shared humanity and our communal experience of life. For we all suffer and we all die, and in the end, there is no reason in the world why something that happened to another person was bound to happen to him rather than to me. The feeling of compassion allows us to experience a strong connection with all other beings. A Buddhist would say that what we have in common is just that we are all capable of suffering. We all have the same basic need for happiness, and for living a decent life, but whereas someone else's good fortune may actually alienate us by provoking envy and personal dissatisfaction—why couldn't that be me?—shared sorrow brings people together, and to a great extent, it allows them to forget their differences.

We must distinguish compassion from other related ideas. Compassion is by no means the same thing as empathy or pity, and even though these are often considered to be synonymous with compassion, they are different, and understanding the differences between them will help to bring out the true meaning of compassion itself. First, empathy is a term that was originally coined in 1909, and it means "to feel one's way into the feelings of another." For example, I may empathize with you if you have to take an exam because I know what taking an exam feels like, and so—in a sense—I feel your pain. But the fact is, I am not taking an exam at the moment, and there might be other situations in which I feel badly for you, but I cannot claim to have experienced what you are suffering now. If you are mourning a child, but I have never had children, I can still feel compassion for your loss. I can also feel compassion for someone who has gone mad, or died young, even though I have no idea of what these experiences would be like. So even though I feel compassion, I cannot always feel empathy, and this implies that compassion and empathy must be different. In compassion, I feel for the other person who is suffering, or in a bad situation. Her lack of well-being affects me and deflects me from my habitual self-absorption. But I don't need to suffer with her or feel the same way that she does to feel compassion for her. Empathy involves putting myself in the place of the other to such an extent that the difference between self and other seems to collapse. Sometimes when I say, "I feel your pain," I really mean what I say, and this suggests a blurring of the boundaries between myself and the other person. The whole point about compassion, however, is that even though it promotes identification between myself and the other, it never destroys the difference between us. In fact, true compassion involves respecting the other person as the one who is suffering *now*.

Pity is also sadness for another person's unhappiness or unhappy situation. But pity usually implies contempt. Pity is a "vertical" relationship in which we tend to look down on another whom we no longer respect. "I could pity you" implies that you are beneath me. But compassion requires respect. It is a horizontal relationship—a relationship of equals—in which I demonstrate respect for the other person by showing my concern for her. In compassion I am not just a spectator; I bear witness to her suffering—and as we have noted, such compassion involves bringing the other person back to the community that she has been alienated from. When another person has suffered a great misfortune or bereavement, we are concerned to show commiseration, and concern and commiseration are the signs of our respect.

Finally, we should add that compassion implies passivity, which belongs to its etymology, as *com-pathein*, meaning *to suffer, undergo or experience with*. And since compassion takes its lead from the other person, it would seem to be a kind of reactive sadness which is evoked regardless of my personal wishes. At the same time, it also makes sense to think of compassion as the most basic kind of receptivity to others. For without compassion and the openness to the other that compassion implies, we remain closed off to anything that is different, and indeed to anything that is greater than we are. Hence we can say that compassion is original responsiveness and the basic condition for spiritual enhancement and growth. It is "passive" in one sense, and yet it is also *openness* to the other person, which allows for generosity and the active dimension of spiritual life.

Bringing all of these ideas together, we may now define compassion as *sorrow for the suffering of another and the desire to relieve her distress*. We may not always be able to relieve someone else's distress, and there may be stronger impulses (usually selfish ones) that prevent us from helping every time. But a part of us, at least, is not indifferent to that person's suffering, and this implies that we have a basic impulse to do whatever we can to help someone who is suffering before us. In this respect, compassion is definitely more than a feeling since it involves reflection on the means of alleviating suffering in any given case. It also leads to a new perspective that draws us away from the selfish ego and its desires, and as we will see in the final part of this chapter, by *cultivating* compassion, we may reach a point of openness and concern for suffering wherever it occurs.

PHILOSOPHERS AND COMPASSION

We can now return to the history of philosophy and consider some of the reasons why philosophers—and non-philosophers—have been reluctant to accept compassion as a fundamental virtue. The Stoics, Kant, and Nietzsche all look down on pity as something that should be avoided, and Nietzsche goes out of his way to condemn pity as one of

the worst things. In *The Antichrist* he comments, "Pity stands opposed
to the tonic emotions which heighten our vitality: it has a depressing
effect. We are deprived of strength when we feel pity. That loss of
strength which suffering as such inflicts on life is still further increased
and multiplied by pity. Pity makes suffering contagious."[16] Of course,
there may be problems with pity (which is by no means the same thing
as compassion, although it is related to it), but all the same, the vehe-
mence of Nietzsche's attack on pity draws attention to itself. Given the
prevalence of cruelty, selfishness, and suffering in general, why would
he want to claim that *pity* is such a significant problem? Can we ever
have too much compassion? Like many other philosophers (and non-
philosophers), Nietzsche views emotional responses such as pity and
compassion as forms of weakness rather than strength. But in Buddhism and Christianity, compassion *is* viewed as a sign of strength
because compassion involves the ability to overcome everyday selfishness in order to be with others and to be concerned about their lives.

Could it be that pity and compassion are emotions which undermine
the critical distance that philosophy requires? And could it be—as the
Stoics maintained—that we should give the rule to ourselves; we must
always act, but never simply react to stimuli that we feel, for in this
way we can maintain our own personal *sovereignty*? Nietzsche argues
that pity (like compassion) involves being directed by the emotional
appeal of another, and so it threatens our autonomy and it makes us
dependent on other people. We must take such criticisms seriously, but
even at this point it can be argued that *reason* should not be understood
in a purely instrumental sense. Reason is not necessarily opposed to the
passions (or emotions) such as compassion or love, since the latter may
be one way in which we achieve a greater understanding of the world,
and in this sense, both love and compassion can be considered forms of
wisdom. Some philosophers (and non-philosophers) seem to be afraid
of "letting go" and may worry about losing their autonomy and independence, but authentic spirituality may *require* "letting go" since it
involves a basic trust in the world, in nature, or "the other." Philosophy
has always embraced the fundamental priority of rational reflection. In
fact, it has defined itself in opposition to myth and religion, which
affirm the priority of acceptance and faith. But this means that anything
which appears to challenge the rule of reason must be viewed with
profound suspicion from a philosophical point of view. Love, compassion, and desire are all based on impulses which can overwhelm reason—we sometimes say that love is a kind of madness, and clearly pity

and compassion can cause us to act sentimentally rather than reasonably. For all of these reasons, we must now look at some of the arguments against compassion that have appeared in the history of Western thought. Not *all* Western philosophers have challenged compassion, however, and the philosophical account that we offer in this chapter suggests that philosophy can still illuminate compassion as a spiritual goal.

First, as we saw in the previous chapter, the Stoics believe that we cannot do anything about fate, when and where we were born, or what we encounter in our lives. But we can choose how we respond to anything that happens to us. This at least is within our control, and so the most fundamental distinction lies in the difference between what is in our power and what is not. We must learn to accept whatever happens without rancor or even excitement as "nature," or the will of the cosmos. We must also maintain complete self-mastery by acting virtuously and not consenting to anything that would undermine the inner citadel of the self. But if the Stoic distinction between what is in my power and what is not in my power is very tightly maintained, then compassion becomes problematic because it makes the well-being of others a conditional aspect of my own well-being; and this challenges the self-other distinction that Stoics are bound to maintain. In compassion, I care about others, I am affected by them, and I take their needs seriously. But this undermines the rigid distinction between what belongs to the self (or what is in my power), and what belongs to others. In the case of compassion, the Stoics are very clear—it is all right to show mercy or give material assistance to others, but to pity the afflicted is to weaken self-mastery by taking one's lead from something outside of oneself. Seneca, for example, argues that pity is an unmanly vice that can lead us to abandon whatever is right and good. He goes so far as to say that a wise man does not grieve. He will be respectful in mourning, but he will retain his inner composure and complete self-mastery: "A mind cannot be both great and also grieving, since grief blunts the wits, debases and shrivels them. And that is something that will not happen to a wise man even in his own misfortunes. On the contrary, he will beat back fortune's anger and break it at his feet. He will always have the same calm, unshaken expression, which he could not do if he were open to sadness."[17] Hence, compassion is to be avoided because like other forms of emotional response it undermines our self-control.

Kant is an heir to the Stoic tradition, and he is sympathetic to the Stoic point of view. He says we are bound to follow the moral law, which is also the law of reason. According to Kant, we can't choose what happens to us, but we can choose how we will act—we can will to act in accordance with reason or we can choose to do something bad by making an exception of ourselves to the moral law. From this perspective, compassion is an emotion; it cannot be a virtue because it belongs to our physical nature, and it is not something that is up to us. To emphasize this point, Kant makes a distinction between acting from principle and acting out of loving-kindness. He affirms the first while he disdains the latter since it depends upon a passing feeling:

> Yet I maintain that . . . such an action of this kind [one performed out of sympathy], however right and however amiable it may be, has no genuinely moral worth. It stands on the same footing as other inclinations—for example, the inclination for honour, which if fortunate enough to hit on something beneficial and right and consequently honourable, deserves praise and encouragement, but not esteem; for its maxim lacks moral content, namely, the performance of such actions, not from inclination, but from duty. [18]

In this way, Kant affirms the Stoic position which projects autonomy or self-mastery as the highest goal. Compassion undermines self-mastery, and so it is by no means unconditionally good. Elsewhere, he confirms this point when he notes, "The principle of apathy, that is, that the prudent man must at no time be in a state of emotion, not even of sympathy [*mitleid*] with the woes of his best friend, is an entirely correct and sublime precept of the stoic school because emotions make one (more or less) blind." [19] Hence, there may be some circumstances in which feeling compassion for others would be a mistake. But Kant goes on to argue that sometimes compassion is not only useless, it is actually worse than useless since it creates more misery in the world: "When another suffers and, although I cannot help him, I let myself be infected by his pain (through my imagination), then two of us suffer, though the evil really (in nature) affects only one. But there cannot be a duty to increase the evil in the world and so to do good from compassion." [20] Only right action can help in such a situation, and the agent's emotional condition is irrelevant. So compassion must be avoided; it only multiplies the amount of suffering in the world, and this suggests it may even be a vice.

As we have seen, Nietzsche also regards pity (*mitleid*) as a form of weakness, although it is doubtful whether he would accept that there is a significant distinction between pity and compassion. His most famous attack appears in *The Antichrist*, where he condemns pity as the essence of contemporary *nihilism*:

> Pity is the *practice* of nihilism. To repeat: this depressive and contagious instinct crosses those instincts which aim at the preservation of life and at the enhancement of its value. It multiplies misery and conserves all that is miserable, and is thus a prime instrument of the advancement of decadence: pity persuades men to *nothingness*! Of course, one does not say "nothingness" but "beyond" or "God," or "*true* life," or nirvana, salvation, blessedness."[21]

In this passage, Nietzsche argues that the Christian (and Buddhist) impulse of pity and compassion bring us down to the same level as those who are afflicted and sick of life. But the *overman* is the goal of the future, and so *we* should take charge of our lives and not be distracted by the needs of others. Hence, compassion is not a virtue—it is a vice—because it takes us away from ourselves and the ultimate duty we have to perfect our individual being. Pity and compassion are to be avoided because they promote weakness. The one who pities is corrupted while the one who is pitied is insulted and made to feel contemptible.

What is striking about all these criticisms of compassion is the philosopher's fear of losing self-control. It is the fear of being weak, the fear of emotional disclosure and emotional connection with others, and the fear of self-abandonment. But these are qualities that are really opposed to the opening up of our spiritual life. The Stoic, for example, retreats to the inner citadel of the ego in order to protect himself from the absolute flux of the world. But this is avoidance of love and fear of any real connection with others. Kant's preference for coldhearted goodness is chilling because it reduces ethical life, and caring for others, to a series of impersonal duties that we are bound to observe even if we are angry and resentful about it. In this view, morality is a burden, and it is at odds with personal fulfillment. Nietzsche's attack on pity is polemical and meant to shake up some nineteenth-century platitudes about caring for those who are less fortunate than we are. But Nietzsche also assumes (wrongly) that there is a fundamental opposition between self and other, and that we cannot affirm the one without neglecting the other. He doesn't seem to realize that in the end, caring for others may actually be a way of enhancing our own life. In fact, it would be true to say that we *cultivate* selfhood through our involvement and interaction with other people.

So let us now respond to the philosophical objections to compassion, in order to establish the truth of compassion as the opening of spiritual life. First, *compassion undermines self-control*: this suggests that compassion is associated with self-loss. But another way of thinking about this would be to say that compassion *enlarges* the self by making us more open to the reality of other people's lives, and in this way, compassion leads to self-fulfillment. Compassion mingles our needs with the needs of others in a way that transcends our ordinary "self-interest"—and so it enlarges our sense of who we are. Kant is afraid that compassion may undermine the rule of reason. To this it may be said that compassion is by no means unreasonable or irrational. And just because compassion has an emotional aspect, it does not mean that it is opposed to reason. Compassion is a reasonable emotion because it can be cultivated along rational lines. In fact, it is probably the basis of our ethical life, for without compassion our rational duties wouldn't have the power to move us. As the Dalai Lama notes:

> We find that in practice, if we are not able to connect with others to some extent, if we cannot at least imagine the potential impact of our actions on others, then we have no means to discriminate between right and wrong, between what is appropriate and what is not, between harming and non-harming. It follows, therefore, that if we could enhance this capacity—that is to say, our sensitivity toward others' suffering—the more we did so, the less we could tolerate seeing others' pain and the more we would be concerned to ensure that no action of ours caused harm to others.[22]

Compassion is the basis of morality and the locus of self-fulfillment. It cannot be viewed as self-abandonment in any negative sense.

Second, *compassion multiplies the amount of suffering in the world*. This implies that if you can't actually help someone then just to show compassion is pointless. But, compassion is *itself* the acknowledgement of another person's suffering, and this recognition can be the most important thing since it serves to relieve the sense of isolation of the one who is suffering and affirms her place in the community. It is also not the case that the suffering of compassion is debilitating in the same way that ordinary suffering is, since compassion for another is actually a manifestation of inner strength. Thus, when the *bodhisattva* takes upon himself all the sufferings of the world, this is not a burden that destroys him, but the sign of his enhanced spiritual power. And hence,

> There is an important qualitative distinction to be made between experiencing one's own suffering and experiencing suffering in the course of sharing in others'. In the case of one's own suffering, given that it is involuntary, there is a sense of oppression: it seems to come from outside us. By contrast, sharing in someone else's suffering must at some level involve a degree of voluntariness, which itself is indicative of a certain inner strength. For this reason, the disturbance it may cause is considerably less likely to paralyze us than our own suffering. [23]

People who live compassionate lives seem to radiate calmness and a spiritual peace that is both moving and contagious. For compassion is like love—the more we feel, the more we have to give, and the more empowered we become.

Finally, *compassion promotes weakness*: once again, this presupposes an absolute separation between self and other that is difficult to maintain. Is being responsive to others really just a sign of weakness and an inability to live with oneself? On the contrary, such compassion involves the strength of availability and a readiness to help others that comes from the refusal to remain self-absorbed or self-contained. Do we lose ourselves through involvement with others? It is more likely that through involvement with others we become stronger and more open to all the vicissitudes of life. And if we want to talk about the "sovereignty" of the individual, the ideal of a higher type of human being, or even the overman, then such sovereignty may be achieved, paradoxically, by the refusal to care about personal sovereignty, or the refusal to cling to one's own life as the most important thing.

ENHANCING COMPASSION

As we have noted, Buddhism celebrates compassion as the supreme emotion, and the highest virtue, because it is basic responsiveness to other beings, and as such, it is the precondition for the other virtues, such as courage, sincerity, generosity, and justice. But in this respect, (Buddhist) compassion is more than just empathy or feeling sorry for someone. As we have seen, compassion (*karuna*) is actually the deepest wisdom concerning ultimate reality since it acknowledges the error of the independent ego and affirms the interdependence and interconnectedness of all things. To conclude this discussion of the spiritual aspects of compassion, we may now return to the Buddhist perspective, and particularly the Dalai Lama's account of the different stages of compassion, and the ways of cultivating compassion as a response to suffering. Since Buddhist philosophers have spent so much time reflecting on the spirituality of compassion, we may expect their conclusions to be insightful. Indeed, it makes sense to think of Buddhism as a wisdom tradition since it enjoins a way of living in this world which is supposed to lead to happiness. According to Buddhism, compassion allows us to experience our affinity and our connection with all creatures; and the more committed and involved with others we become, the less preoccupied we are with our own selfish desires. As we cultivate our sense of compassion, the deep concerns and anxieties that characterize our everyday existence fall away, and we become more open to other people and the rhythm of life itself. Such compassion involves an overall attentiveness and availability to the other person. Following Buddhist teaching, it should be unconditional, undifferentiated, and universal in scope, and it would certainly include compassion toward oneself.

Many of the Dalai Lama's writings have centered on the theme of compassion. In various books he has not only insisted on the importance of compassion as the focus of moral life, but he has also discussed techniques for fostering and developing compassion within the individual soul so that it becomes the fundamental aspect of who we are. In *How to Expand Love*, for example, the Dalai Lama describes three different levels of compassion. In the first stage, the individual learns the seed of compassion. For instance, when a parent asks a child how she would feel in someone else's place, she may begin to feel what someone else feels. This is empathy, but empathy is just the beginning of compassion and not its fully-fledged form. In the next stage, one puts altruistic intentions into practice. But, as the Dalai Lama points out, this requires continual effort and one may become discouraged because "it is not easy to help even one sentient being overcome the manifest form of even one type of problem, not to mention overcoming its latent predispositions in the mind. Such improvement requires continuous effort."[24] But if the practitioner perseveres, in spite of all the difficulties she encounters, her commitment to be compassionate will increase.

All of this practice leads ultimately to the final stage of compassion which is referred to in Tibetan as *nying je chenmo*, the great compas-

sion. At this level, a compassionate person will always be fully engaged in the welfare of other individuals and has overcome her sense of
being a self whose interests are separate from all others. Using "skillful
means," the practitioner will show compassion to others in a way that is
consistent with their needs and circumstances. Once again, the Dalai
Lama explains:

> When we enhance our sensitivity toward others suffering through delib-
> erately opening ourselves up to it, it is believed that we can gradually
> extend our compassion to the point where the individual feels so moved
> by even the subtlest suffering of others that they come to have an
> overwhelming sense of responsibility towards those others. This causes
> the one who is compassionate to dedicate themselves entirely to helping
> others overcome both their suffering and the causes of their suffering.[25]

Of course, sharing in the suffering of another person does not mean that
one approves of his or her actions. It simply means that one refuses to
regard anybody's suffering as a matter of indifference. And at no point
is *any* kind of suffering deemed to be irrelevant.

We must never regard our emotional responses as in any way fixed
or inevitable, for these are things that can be cultivated by the skilled
practitioner. Buddhism, like Stoicism, is full of imaginative exercises
that are meant to help us foster good qualities like compassion, or
overwhelm bad qualities such as anger or despair. In Stoicism, we are
told to imagine our own death or the death of our loved ones so that
when these things happen we will not be overwhelmed since we anticipated them before they actually happened. Likewise, in Buddhism, in
the ancient works of Buddhaghosa or Nagarjuna, or the contemporary
writings of the Dalai Lama, we are asked to contemplate the suffering
of a loved one, then the suffering of someone we feel neutral toward,
and finally the suffering of an enemy. In each case, we reflect: "Like
me, this person wants happiness and does not want suffering, yet is
stricken with such pain. May this person be free from suffering and the
causes of suffering!"[26] Proceeding in this way we can eventually feel
what it is like to feel strong compassion. The Dalai Lama emphasizes
the importance of sustained reflection upon this theme: "To me, this
suggests that by means of . . . familiarization with compassion, through
rehearsal and practice we can develop our innate ability to connect with
others, a fact which is of supreme importance given the approach to
ethics I have described. The more we develop compassion, the more
genuinely ethical our conduct will be."[27] Other spiritual techniques

would include *tonglen,* or the practice of exchanging breath (described in the introduction), and sustained meditation on breathing, which involves reflection on the inbreath and the outbreath to promote awareness of transience and the fragility of all life.

The Buddhist writer Stephen Batchelor emphasizes how the cultivation of compassion requires continual vigilance and mindful awareness. Perhaps this is not a goal that can ever be fully achieved, but it is possible to make continual progress toward it:

> The selfless vulnerability of compassion requires the vigilant protection of mindful awareness. It is not enough to *want* to feel this way toward others. We need to be alert at all times to the invasion of thoughts and emotions that threaten to break in and steal this open and caring result. A compassionate heart still feels anger, greed, jealousy, and other such emotions. But it accepts them for what they are with equanimity, and cultivates the strength of mind to let them arise and pass without identifying with or acting upon them.[28]

We cannot always prevent the upsurge of negative thoughts and emotions, but we don't have to identify with these mental contents. The feeling of anger is just that—it does not have to be embraced as *mine*, and it will go away if I simply observe it as something that emerges inside of me. The feeling of compassion, on the other hand, should be evoked and enhanced since it is a positive response. In this way, Buddhism, like Stoicism and other ancient philosophies, achieves a profound enhancement of spiritual life, and it offers the most appropriate reaction to suffering in the cultivation of compassion as spiritual wisdom and ethical response. As the original openness to the other, compassion is also the condition for generosity and the active dimension of spiritual life, and this is what we must now discuss.

Chapter Three

Generosity

Generosity is a moral virtue, and people can be generous, extravagant, or mean. But it is also possible to view life itself as a principle of generosity: the universe is abundant, and showing gratitude for what we have been given is a fundamental spiritual attitude. Poets and philosophers have responded to the generosity of the world in different ways. The poets celebrate the generosity of life by showing how the things of this world—the sea, the rose, the panther, and human love—must be appreciated for their own sake. The poets make us aware of things that we may not have noticed before, and poetry cherishes the particular. Philosophers, on the other hand, have been more critical of those perspectives which seem to be emotional or attitudinal instead of being rationally grounded. Philosophers deal in concepts, and so they are less open to the immediacy of life. Indeed, the concept of "the given" is something that contemporary philosophers hold at arm's length. The world is always mediated by concepts—or so it is said— and philosophy is typically limited to concepts that are a pale imitation of reality.

To grasp the sheer generosity of life can be an overwhelming experience which cannot be placed at a critical distance, for in a sense life always gives itself; it is the benefactor and we are its beneficiaries. We don't deserve these things in any absolute way, and we must disabuse ourselves of any sense of entitlement. Of course, there will always be suffering, death, and mourning, but unless we are completely traumatized, the underlying goodness of the world forms a part of our ordinary experience of it, and it makes us want to go on living. And so we learn to enjoy life, and we cultivate everyday pleasures associated with friendship, nature, beauty, and learning. This is not another attempt to restore theodicy, which was rejected in the chapter on suffering, but it serves to underline the importance of gratitude as a basic spiritual attitude.

The religious response to all this is to give thanks and to give praise since gift giving seems to imply a giver. But philosophers, even those with religious beliefs, have largely ignored the generosity of life as a possible theme for rational reflection. There are a few exceptions—Nietzsche, Heidegger, and Derrida all have a strong sense of the generosity of life, and in their work they dwell on the possibility of the gift. Heidegger writes, "es gibt," meaning that Being gives itself. He also writes, "denken ist danken," thinking is thanking, which suggests that thoughtful reflection is itself an expression of our gratitude to the world.[1] From this perspective, philosophy is not about problem solving at all, since it illuminates the goodness of Being. But if we don't recognize this fundamental generosity and respond to it accordingly, we remain closed off from the possibilities of spiritual life.

From a more typical philosophical perspective most claims about the "generosity of life" are spurious because they can't be proved or because they seem to presuppose "life" as some kind of impersonal subject. Philosophers are also more accustomed to dealing with generosity as an ethical theme rather than a spiritual one. Bearing this in mind, we shall therefore begin the discussion of generosity by specifying three defining features of generous actions, and from this point we can move from the ethical to the spiritual level. First, generosity must involve the desire to benefit someone else. If I give something to you, it is not a generous action if my goal is to impress you or make you feel indebted. The generous action isn't done for the sake of future repayment, since this would make it self-interested after all. This means that generosity involves a focus on the needs and desires of the other person, since I cannot benefit someone if I don't know what they need. Giving a child the most expensive toy is not necessarily a generous action, especially if I don't take the time to find out what she really wants. Giving someone money to buy drugs is not a generous action either because it shows an indifference to the other's well-being that is not consistent with the spirit of generosity. The second point is that generosity must involve giving away something that I value. I am not being generous if I pass on some old clothes that I might just as easily have thrown away, and it's not a generous action if I choose to sacrifice my life for someone else because I no longer want to live. The paradox is that generosity seems to involve an awareness of what it is that one has given, and yet we tend to think that a really generous person is oblivious to the time or money she has chosen to spend on others—she empties her wallet for a homeless person, or she is willing to help someone who is fleeing from persecution. The important point is that she gives or helps without counting the cost or making a calculation based on self-interest; but this doesn't mean that she doesn't care about money or her own life. Finally, generosity involves giving that is *excessive* insofar as it goes beyond whatever is required by duty or what the other person can reasonably expect or deserve. It is not a generous action to repay a debt, although it may be a just one. And it is not always a generous action to give money to a good cause, although it would be if one gave away everything one had since this goes far beyond what is typically required.[2]

The last point is especially important. One of the most significant things about generosity is how it is tied to that which is *not necessary*. No one can be required or obligated to be generous, because generosity only exists insofar as it goes beyond whatever is required. That is why generous actions will always be surprising, since they are unexpected and derive from the complete spontaneity of life. And the generous action is also an expression of freedom insofar as it is not constrained in any way. Generosity may at first appear to be a secondary virtue and a luxury, or one that isn't really required. But on closer reflection it seems to be the animating condition of the other virtues and the principle of their fulfillment, for it is the point at which the individual gives herself to the other, and, for a while at least, she overcomes the limitations of individual selfhood. In this respect, generosity belongs to the active dimension of spiritual life, which involves self-overcoming in the fullest sense.

Generosity is the virtue connected with giving. Initially, we assume that generous actions involve the gift of material goods; and when Aristotle discusses liberality and magnificence in Book Four of the *Nicomachean Ethics*, he reflects the popular belief that a generous person is simply one who gives money and goods to others, albeit to the right people, at the right time, and for the right reasons. But there are other kinds of generosity. People can be generous with their time as well as their money, and they can cultivate a generous attitude toward others and overlook their failings. People can interpret other people's actions in the best possible light that is still consistent with reality. And in the spirit of generosity they can also forgive a wrong to allow the offender to get on with her life. These are all spiritual attitudes that reflect a kind of attunement to the goodness of the world, and in this sense, forgiveness, gratitude (giving thanks), and the refusal to be mean-spirited are among those actions that reflect true generosity of spirit, or self-overcoming for the sake of someone else.

In this chapter, we begin with the traditional perspective on generosity, by looking at two philosophers, Aristotle and Nietzsche, who explore generosity in their accounts of "liberality" and the "gift-giving virtue" respectively. Aristotle thinks of generosity as a measured ethical virtue, while for Nietzsche, the gift-giving virtue is a reflection of the fecundity of the universe which cannot be moderated or contained. Next, we shall look at another model of generosity that is focused on *caring*. Caring is the opposite of self-assertion; it involves a kind of withdrawal of oneself for the sake of the other person and loving attention to what *she* needs in order to flourish. The first account of generosity leads to a discussion of *affirmation, availability*, and *openness* as different aspects of spiritual generosity, while *caring* is shown to be self-overcoming for the sake of someone else, and it lies at the heart of our spiritual life.

ARISTOTLE AND GENEROSITY

Human beings tend to be selfish. They care about themselves and those they are close to, but they don't always desire the well-being of everyone else. We need the virtues because they encourage us to care about each other, and we praise people for being courageous, prudent, and generous because we don't routinely act in this way. In the *Nicomachean Ethics*, Aristotle offers a systematic account of the virtues, including generosity (and magnificence), which are the qualities of a good human being. For Aristotle, virtue is all about practical judgment or *phronesis*. To be generous simply means that you know how and when to give in the most appropriate way. This requires calculation and a sense of measure, and it means that the truly generous person can never really lose himself or give himself away unless the sacrifice is considered reasonable or worth it. Aristotle's account of generosity seems to be supported by popular opinion or "common sense," for it does seem possible to give too little or too much, and we must admit that generosity is just a *part* of our ethical life.

In his *Ethics*, Aristotle locates generosity (or liberality) as a mean between the two vices of prodigality and meanness, and he claims that it denotes the proper attitude toward wealth:

> Virtuous actions are fine, and are done for a fine end; so the liberal man too will give with a fine end in view, and in the right way; because he will give to the right people, and the right amounts, and at the right time, and will observe all the other conditions that accompany right giving. And he will have pleasure, or at least no pain, in doing this; because a virtuous act is pleasant or painless, but certainly not painful. [3]

By contrast, the illiberal man is someone who accumulates money and property for its own sake, regardless of whether it benefits the household or the community. And as Aristotle notes, "We always ascribe illiberality to persons who take money too seriously."[4] Elsewhere, in the *Politics*, Aristotle seems to despise those who accumulate wealth pointlessly and beyond their actual needs. Such people overvalue wealth; they make a fetish out of it, and this diminishes their excellence as human beings.[5] On the other hand, there are those who waste their capital on trifles or give it away to others because they don't have any sense of the value of money. Significantly, Aristotle adds that such people enjoy spending, and they are not much bothered about where their money comes from. And so they become indebted, which undermines the (masculine) ideal of independence and self-reliance. By contrast, the truly generous man enjoys giving—he doesn't cling to everything that he has, but he is also very prudent, and he doesn't waste his money on foolish expenses. He takes care to maintain his property so that he will continue to have something to give.

Aristotle discusses generosity (or "liberality") at the beginning of Book Four of the *Nicomachean Ethics*; then he focuses more specifically on magnificence, which he views as liberality on a spectacular scale; and finally he offers his famous portrait of the *megalopsychos,* the *magnanimous* or "great-souled" man. The magnanimous man is meant to epitomize the virtuous ideal, and Aristotle regards him as one whose magnificence of spirit raises him high above ordinary people. In fact, Aristotle's discussion of liberality and magnificence in gift giving culminates with the account of the magnanimous man, who refuses to be indebted to anyone in any way and who is, consequently, the most self-sufficient person: "He is not prone to express admiration, because nothing is great in his eyes. He does not nurse resentment, because it is beneath a magnanimous man to remember things against people, especially wrongs; it is more like him to overlook them. He does not care for personal conversation; he will talk neither about himself nor about anyone else, because he does not care to be complimented himself or to hear others criticized; nor again is he inclined to pay compliments."[6]

Aristotle emphasizes that the magnanimous man has the proper estimate of his own worth. He is not falsely modest, and neither is he arrogant or boastful but properly deserving. This ideal figure is the embodiment of solidity and he is clearly self-contained, even to the point of being "slow-moving," because he isn't excitable and doesn't immediately respond to everything that happens; he also speaks in a low voice, which reflects his obvious reserve. Aristotle says that the magnanimous man is not concerned with money or any other base motivations but primarily with honor: "Indeed it is apparent even without argument that magnanimous people are concerned with honour, because it is honour above all that they claim as their due, and deservedly."[7] But then, he appears to correct himself when he points out that the magnanimous man is unmoved by tributes from those who are beneath him: "At great honours bestowed by responsible persons he will feel pleasure, but only a moderate one, because he will feel that he is getting no more than his due, or rather less, since no honour can be enough for perfect excellence. Nevertheless, he will accept such honours, on the ground that there is nothing greater that they can give him."[8]

Aristotle's magnanimous man is supposed to be the embodiment of generosity (and all the other virtues), but he appears to be disdainful and imbued with a strong sense of his own self-importance. He is ready to give his life, but only if the cause is great enough. Presumably, he is concerned about making a grand gesture and he doesn't want to waste the opportunity with a cause that is too paltry. Likewise, he prefers to forget that he has ever been benefited or indebted to others, while he never allows those that *he* has benefited to forget. He is usually indifferent to other people because they are beneath his notice; he doesn't care what they think about him, and he doesn't seek out partners or praise other people for their achievements. And a sign of his honorable or excellent nature is, paradoxically, that he doesn't seem to *strive* for honors or excellence. As Aristotle notes, "He does not enter for popular contests, or ones in which others distinguish themselves; he hangs back or does nothing at all, except where the honour or the feat is a great one. The tasks that he undertakes are few, but grand and celebrated."[9]

In the end, this specifically masculine figure of independence and self-sufficiency seems to undermine itself as an attractive community virtue. And we might ask, to what extent does this great-souled man really need the community that he belongs to? He doesn't need their honors, and he is basically indifferent to most of his contemporaries. Perhaps he only needs the community indirectly, as a forum in which his virtues can shine. In any case, while Aristotle insists that such a man is by definition the apogee of all virtue, this man is also self-absorbed, and in some ways, he is the opposite of the generous spirit who gives himself for other people. The magnanimous man *would* give himself for others if the cause were great enough—or if this produced an appropriate spectacle—but it's not clear if he would give himself for any other reason. The paradox, then, is that even while he does noble deeds, the magnanimous man holds onto himself. He is unwilling to give himself away, and he retains a strong sense of his own distinction and what is owed to him. But he is not generous in the deepest sense which would require forgetting about even these things. We will see a similar ambivalence about generosity in Nietzsche's account of the gift-giving virtue: Aristotle's discussion of the magnanimous man is inspired by an ideal of generosity and inner strength, but by insisting on self-sufficiency and personal distinction, he gives us an individual who cannot overcome himself except in the most spectacular forms of self-sacrifice. There is something wrong with this discussion of generosity, even though it is the most influential theory and supposedly the reflection of "common sense." Nietzsche's account of the gift-giving virtue further illuminates the possibility of spiritual generosity, but it also involves self-assertion, and in this respect it leads us toward a different point of view.

NIETZSCHE ON THE GIFT-GIVING VIRTUE

Generosity is a significant theme in Nietzsche's writings, and gift giving is a recurrent motif. At the start of *Thus Spoke Zarathustra*, for example, whoever disdains self-preservation and opens himself up to the energies of life is praised as a bridge to the *overman*, or Nietzsche's ideal of the future. As Zarathustra puts it, "I love him whose soul squanders itself, who wants no thanks and returns none: for he always gives himself away and does not want to preserve himself."[10] Zarathustra makes much of the generosity involved in "giving oneself away," and a similar sense of the absolute generosity of the universe inspires his teaching of the *eternal recurrence*: it seems that the most well-disposed individual is the one who can affirm everything that happens, and wants it to recur over and over again, innumerable times more. In contrast to Aristotle, Nietzsche seems to repudiate the prudential calculation of liberality, or the very idea that someone could be *too* generous. For Nietzsche, generosity has to be an extreme act of squandering and sacrifice that does not keep itself out of play or calculate its own advantage. The generosity of the world is unlimited and the highest virtue; the gift-giving virtue must also be unbounded.

Much of Nietzsche's thinking about generosity is given at the end of the first part of *Thus Spoke Zarathustra*, which Nietzsche claims is his "gift" to mankind and his most important work. *Thus Spoke Zarathustra* is a strange book, written in a parabolic style, and while it is a profoundly spiritual work, it is also open to a variety of different interpretations. In what follows, we shall focus on the section called "On the gift-giving virtue," which is a parable concerning the nature of virtue and the true meaning of generosity. Here, for example, Zarathustra addresses his followers:

> Verily, I have found you out, my disciples: you strive, as I do, for the gift-giving virtue. What would you have in common with cats and wolves? This is your thirst: to become sacrifices and gifts yourselves; and that is why you thirst to pile up all the riches in your soul. Insatiably your soul strives for treasures and gems, because your virtue is insatiable in wanting to give. You force all things to and into yourself that they may flow back out of your well as the gifts of your love. Verily, such a gift-giving love must approach all values as a robber; but whole and holy I call this selfishness.[11]

The meaning of the text is not immediately apparent. But as with any parable, we must aim for a creative interpretation which is justified insofar as it incorporates the teaching into the context of our lives. Such an interpretation must also be in accord with the spirit of Nietzsche's philosophy.

In the passage quoted above, the "gift-giving virtue" is treated as a principle of pure abundance: it bestows itself; like the overman, or the sun, it illuminates everything with its own light. In the same way, Zarathustra praises his disciples for wanting to make themselves "sacrifices and gifts," but here the emphasis is entirely on *giving* with no consideration of how the gift will be received. As we have seen, we typically think of giving as other-directed: I give you what you need, and what I give must be of value to both of us, or I can hardly be considered generous. For Zarathustra, however, the gift-giving virtue follows more directly from the correct attunement to life: "When your heart flows broad and full like a river, a blessing and a danger to those living near: there is the origin of your virtue."[12] This means that the gift-giving virtue is "selfish" insofar as it expresses the exuberance of life in its highest examples, such as the overman or even Zarathustra, and this may be inspiring to others, including the disciples, who benefit from such a "gift." As Nietzsche explains elsewhere, to be able to give in this way is "a happiness that, like the sun in the evening, continually bestows its inexhaustible riches, pouring them into the sea, feeling richest, as the sun does, only when even the poorest fisherman is still rowing with golden oars."[13] The gift-giving virtue is "useless" because it cannot be measured in terms of ordinary social utility, but it is also the "highest" virtue because it is an expression of the pure generosity of life, and for Nietzsche there is nothing *beyond* life that could represent a higher achievement.

At the beginning of *Thus Spoke Zarathustra*, Zarathustra says he must leave the mountains because he has become overfull of wisdom: "like a bee that has gathered too much honey; I need hands outstretched to receive it."[14] In this respect, his generosity is a whole and holy "selfishness." The problem, however, is that all of this implies a self-regarding delight in his own power, where the benefit to others is quite secondary or merely coincidental. What seems to be most important is the greatness of the giver rather than the benefit of those who receive his gifts. Nietzsche is very clear that the gift-giving virtue involves giving oneself rather than money or things—the gift-giving virtue is like gold, he explains, which, "always gives itself." And in opposition to Aristotle, the gift-giving virtue doesn't involve any kind of calculation or reckoning—it is a gift-giving virtue precisely because whatever is given is given freely and completely and without the expectation of any kind of return. It would not be a gift if there were strings attached. But can we really call it "generosity" if it derives more from an inner necessity, the need to give, than from the needs of other people? And don't we need to remember that generosity is only a virtue insofar as it is other-directed? To give well, or to be accomplished at the gift-giving virtue, the giver must know what the other person needs or doesn't need; she cannot give too much or too little for she would shame the other person if her gift was excessive, or inappropriate, and this would not be virtuous. Likewise, she must know when to give and how to give her present, but these things depend upon knowing and esteeming the person who is to receive the gift. Giving without reference to the recipient cannot be considered true generosity, and this challenges Zarathustra's initial assertion that the gift-giving virtue is a higher form of *selfishness*.

Zarathustra's early discussion of the gift-giving virtue emphasizes the one who gives and only to a lesser extent the one who receives. As we have seen, the same is also true of Aristotle's account of liberality. The problem, however, is that the act of generosity may then become a kind of spectacle and display. The one who gives never disappears into his action but seems to celebrate and affirm himself in the very act of giving. And yet generosity must be other-directed, since the whole point is to benefit those who are lacking in some respect. And it can be argued that without such an overriding intention, the action cannot be considered generous at all.

Later, Zarathustra becomes more focused on his followers. He is concerned that they should find their *own* way, and so he says to them, "Now I bid you lose me and find yourselves; and only when you have all denied me will I return to you."[15] By sending his disciples away, Zarathustra is forcing them to take charge of their own lives—and this is exactly right, for the teacher of the overman could never be happy with *followers* who obey another's rules and commandments instead of pursuing their *own* way. And so at this point, the goal of the gift-giving virtue becomes associated with the ideal of personal sovereignty, or what Nietzsche later refers to as "how one becomes what one is." It involves helping others to realize their complete potential as human beings, which means inspiring them to become themselves.

But how is this an expression of generosity? And how are we to understand Zarathustra's oracular wisdom on this point? Here, we leave the patient analysis of Nietzsche's text for the more creative appropriation of Nietzsche's ideas. Perhaps the language to describe these things adequately does not exist, but let us think about *availability*, *affirmation*, and *openness* as among the most significant aspects of spiritual generosity which can help to inspire the sovereignty of another person. This is not a complete list, but it serves to begin a discussion, and while my examples may seem prosaic in the context of Zarathu stra's rhetoric, this should not invalidate them as forms of the gift-giving virtue.

First, there is generosity involved in *availability*. Availability means giving someone else one's time or one's focus, not responding to their needs in a merely reactive way, but helping to guide them through their difficulties and even anticipating where difficulties may emerge. The good teacher, the good parent, or the good friend is someone who gives us a strong sense of life's possibilities, and this means freeing us to become who we are. In this respect, Nietzsche thought of himself as an educator. He puts it most clearly in *Beyond Good and Evil*, where he seems to be describing himself:

> The genius of the heart from whose touch everyone goes away richer, not favored and surprised, not as if blessed and oppressed with the goods of others, but richer in himself, newer to himself than before, broken open, blown open and sounded out by a thawing wind, more uncertain perhaps, more delicate, more fragile, more broken but full of hopes that as yet have no names. [16]

In the *Symposium*, Alcibiades says something very similar about the effect of Socrates on his own personal development and the renewal of spiritual possibilities that Socrates inspires. [17] The good teacher leaves us with a love of learning that lasts throughout life. But he or she can only appeal to us in this way by paying very close attention to who we are and what is most likely to interest or inspire us; and this is a skill which depends upon patient concern and availability that is oriented toward the spiritual situation of others.

Next, there is generosity in *affirmation*: the principle of charity requires us to look at things in the best possible light, and the truly generous person will tend to interpret another's actions in the best light that is still consistent with reality. In this way the other person is encouraged with the vision of her own better self, which is given to her as a genuine possibility to pursue. A child caught cheating on a test isn't necessarily "bad"—she may not even appreciate that cheating is wrong; someone who doesn't succeed in his chosen career could be considered unlucky, or perhaps not especially ambitious, rather than a "failure." This is the very opposite of the mean-spirited approach—or "nay-saying"—that finds fault with everything and gives the other person an image of herself as someone who is limited and flawed. Nietzsche has some ironic comments on how to put up with one's fellow human beings, but one point seems to confirm the way of affirmation: "Second principle: to 'improve' one's fellow man, by praise, for example, so that he begins to sweat out his delight in himself, or to grab a corner of his good or 'interesting' qualities and to pull at it until the whole virtue comes out and one can hide one's fellow man in its folds."[18] Giving support and encouragement of any kind are forms of affirmation that help the other person to become who they are—this does not include mindless affirmation, of course, but whatever follows from focused attention and concern for another's well-being. This kind of concern cannot be specified or entailed by any particular actions, and others may disagree with particular choices that I make—but in any case, to care for another person is to give priority to her well-being as if it were my own. Through affirmation I demonstrate my concern, or caring, which allows another to make the most of her life. And it is this concern that she will respond to as a measure of her own perceived worth.

Another expression of spiritual generosity is *openness* (or we could say open-mindedness)—openness to another, whether friend or enemy; openness to the future; or openness to life. This means not insisting that the future should resemble the past, or that another person should stay exactly the same as they have always been; it involves the willingness to embrace change or to accept new possibilities of life which make it easier for another to find herself. One example of this would be a willingness to question your own settled ideas whenever this is called for—especially when the alternative would be to reject another person, dismissively, just for being "wrong." If my friend thinks that something is important, then I am bound to consider it seriously too, even if I previously rejected it as irrelevant or wrong—religious belief, for example, *or* the possibility of atheism. Sometimes, for the sake of love or friendship, I have to overcome my preconceived ways of thinking about the world, and this may be challenging. Nietzsche describes the experience of love as rejoicing in the existence of another person who thinks and feels quite differently than we do, but this could also characterize true generosity of spirit as we have described it so far.[19] It is openness to the other which does not have to insist upon its own point of view.

Nietzsche calls the gift-giving virtue a form of noble *selfishness*, but it cannot be selfishness in any ordinary sense because it must be directed toward others—it involves knowing them and valuing who they are—and in the preliminary analysis of availability, affirmation, and openness, we considered three different aspects of spiritual generosity that Nietzsche would certainly affirm. There are others, of course, including forgiveness, which we will discuss in the next chapter as a more concrete example of generosity in action. Nietzsche's gift-giving virtue involves the profound awareness of the spiritual possibilities of another person and guides her toward the fulfillment of such possibilities without *imposing* any fixed ideas upon her. According to Nietzsche, the gift-giving virtue is the highest virtue of all, and so it is presumably the highest achievement of the self. At the same time, his account of the gift-giving virtue illuminates *the sacred* as that which is excessive and always unexpected, for it is nothing other than the pure generosity of life. But generosity cannot just be a matter of self-affirmation, since it involves the withdrawal of the self for the sake of another; the desire for sovereignty or self-mastery gets in the way of generosity as a virtue in the deepest sense. This suggests another model of generosity which involves self-overcoming rather than self-affirmation, and this is what we must now discuss.

GENEROSITY AS CARING

The "masculine" ideal of generosity which is associated with magnificent gift-giving and the spectacular soul can be contrasted with a "feminine" paradigm of generosity, which offers a more compelling account of spiritual activity through self-overcoming. This new paradigm is rooted in the possibility of *caring* and involves receptivity, responsiveness, and relatedness, or the withdrawal of the everyday self that caring involves. By saying that caring is a feminine model of generosity, I do not mean to imply that only women can properly care for others. Just that the care of others, including children, the sick, and the elderly, usually takes place in the domestic context and until recently women have been largely responsible for this domain of life, and even considered especially suited for it. This attitude has been a source of oppression, since it often requires women to experience their own fulfillment in the domestic routine of caring for others and to regard any other desires as forms of selfishness. But even if the ideal of caring has sometimes been oppressive to the one who cares, it is still a remarkable expression of generosity to put aside one's own personal goals to focus directly on the needs of others. In the end, this model of generosity is more profoundly life affirming than the generous act which leaves the self intact.

The very idea of a "theory" of caring is probably a contradiction in terms, since every caring relationship is different and requires being responsive and responsible to a particular individual who is cherished as unique. It would be wrong to treat all your children in exactly the same way, since this would be to make caring into a matter of technique. The point is to be receptive and responsive to the particular needs of each individual, and not to rely on a set of fixed principles that are supposed to apply to everyone in the same way. As those who discuss caring have often pointed out, the ethical principle, or uniform policy, often gets in the way of authentic caring—if we feel morally obliged to punish every act of defiance or disobedience, we are placing a *principle* above the goal of caring itself, and the result will be counter-productive. For the same reason, we cannot reduce caring to a set of objective rules, although we can consider some of the most basic and distinctive features of caring in its different manifestations. Through the use of examples we can articulate the elements of caring to show how it is an expression of profound generosity.

The first point is that caring involves focused attention on the well-being of the one who is cared for, and it implies a very sensitive concern for that person's needs in all their specificity: to act primarily for her physical, emotional, and spiritual well-being, and to such an extent that our own personal goals and projects may be experienced as secondary by comparison. In her discussion of the mother-child relationship as a paradigm of caring, Nel Noddings describes this attitude as one of *engrossment*, and elsewhere Simone Weil and Iris Murdoch have referred to the same attitude as *attentive love*.[20] The point is, if we really care about our children, then we will not just take care of them in the sense of making sure they are well-fed and receive a decent education. For caring to take place, we must also be effectively involved in their lives. We will be relieved and happy when they are doing well, and saddened, perhaps more than the child herself, when she suffers disappointment: "In caring encounters, I receive the other person and feel what he or she is feeling even if I am quite sure intellectually that I would not myself feel that way in the given situation."[21] Simone Weil writes, "This way of looking is first of all attentive. The soul empties itself of all its own contents in order to receive the being it is looking at, just as he is, in all his truth. Only he who is capable of attention can do this."[22] In the end, this is not a relationship in which self and other remain completely separate. As Noddings points out, in caring, "I set aside my temptation to analyze and to plan. I do not project; I receive the other into myself, and I see and feel with the other. I become a duality."[23] In this respect we could perhaps say that caring is a form of giving that creates relationships between people and emphasizes their connection and community with each other. It does not create a sense of indebtedness that we might associate with Aristotelian liberality or even Zarathustra's idea of the gift-giving virtue.

For some philosophers, especially Nietzsche, there is a deep suspicion that caring and concern for others is really an attempt to flee from oneself. There may be cases where people throw themselves into service work to escape from their problems, and presumably there are some mothers (and fathers) who identify so much with their own children they begin to live vicariously through them—as Freud insists, parental love is basically a form of displaced narcissism.[24] But it is important to emphasize that caring in an authentic sense does not involve the *abandonment* of one's own self. And it is certainly not related to the kind of self-loss that we sometimes associate with romantic love. In caring for a child, for example, we need to be able to put all of our own anxieties and personal desires to one side for the sake of the child whenever she needs our personal attention. But it really doesn't help to relinquish our own existence and all our personal goals, for then we have no inner resources and no place to stand from which we can offer the child our help.

The generosity involved in caring is not a form of self-assertion, but neither is it self-abandonment; it is an active expression of spirit which is accomplished in self-withdrawal. For example, the good parent is one who allows her child to become the best possible person that she can become, which is not achieved by dominating or controlling her or by deciding everything for her. But it is also not achieved by allowing her to do anything she wants, regardless of consequences or danger. It involves guiding her to an independent life of her own, helping her, and acting whenever this is required, but also standing back and letting her be, whenever this would be better. Noddings summarizes this goal:

> The one-caring is engrossed in the cared-for and undergoes a motivational displacement toward the projects of the cared-for. This does not, as we have seen, imply romantic love or the sort of pervasive or compulsive "thinking of the other" that characterizes infatuation. It means, rather, that the one-caring receives the other, for the interval of caring, completely and non-selectively. She is present to the other and places her motive power in his service.[25]

Obviously, this implies not looking at the child as one's own personal possession or as a reflection of one's own former self. And it means not treating the child as an ethical project along with one's other obligations. In this context, caring as a mode of generosity involves giving oneself for another, identifying with her well-being, and knowing when this requires activity and when this requires holding back.

In the end, it must be allowed that caring is a profound manifestation of spiritual generosity: in caring for a child, one does one's best to communicate virtue, one's own sense of the good, and to bring happiness to the child that one cares for. This is not for the sake of any material reward and certainly not to create a debt that must be repaid; it is to continue the cycle of caring of one for another as a pure act of generosity which enhances life and puts us in deep attunement with it. For even though caring may involve incurring personal sacrifice for the sake of another, it is not usually regarded *as* a sacrifice or with any sense of loss. In fact, most parents will testify that caring for children, with the endless round of cooking, doing laundry, and helping with homework, etc., is a deeply fulfilling part of their own life.

The kind of care that parents give their children is not the only kind of caring that exists: we care for our friends by looking after them whenever they need our help, and we give them our time, our physical assistance, and emotional reassurance. Likewise, men and women have to care for partners who have AIDS, Alzheimer's disease, or other disabling conditions, and this involves the most difficult task of respecting the maturity and autonomy of the other person, while at the same time accepting their physical reliance on others. There is clearly a huge difference between caring for a child and caring for someone who is already a mature human being, and the responsiveness of caring must testify to this difference. [26]

Let us now consider a significant example of caring which demonstrates the complete generosity that can be found in such a loving relationship: the writer John Bayley and the philosopher Iris Murdoch were married for many years before Iris developed symptoms of Alzheimer's disease. Her symptoms were slight at first, but later she lost her memory of people and places, and she forgot that she had written twenty-five of the most highly acclaimed books. Little by little she lost her ability to care for herself, and Bayley, in his loving memoir, describes how he continued to love and care for her, even though she was now oblivious to the shared personal history that had been the substance of their relationship together. Bayley is no saint; he periodically gets very angry with Iris, who takes to following him around the house, endlessly repeating the same anxious question: "Is it time to go yet?" He is annoyed when she destroys his plants by compulsively over-watering them, or when she makes a scene on the bus returning from an outing. But in spite of their change in circumstances, he continues to love and care for her. And his caring is focused on her existence, which is unique and certainly irreducible to a given condition or a set of symptoms. As he comments, "One needs very much to feel that the unique individuality of one's spouse has not been lost in the common symptoms of a clinical condition."[27] Bayley's generosity is evident not only in the complete sweep of their relationship together, in choosing to care for Iris alone and for the most part without resentment or anger, but also in small acts of kindness which are accomplished on a daily basis. As he lies beside her, his attentive love and engrossment in her life is abundantly clear: "In the past, she would have been up and in her study, in her own world. I am in mine, but it seems to be hers, too, because of proximity. She murmurs, more or less asleep, and her hand comes out from under the quilt. I put mine on it and stroke her finger-nails for a moment, noticing how long they are, and how dirty. I must cut them and clean them again this morning. They seem to grow faster by the month, and I suppose mine do the same."[28]

In his final years with Iris, recorded with great love and in the spirit of generosity, Bayley describes how in this way he came to negotiate a kind of routine for their everyday life together. In spite of everything, he tried to maintain continuity with the past that would allow both of them to have the fullest kind of life that was possible under the circum-stances. Toward the end, for example, he comments, "We can still talk as we did then, but it doesn't make sense any more, on either side. I can't reply in the way I used to do then, but only in the way she speaks to me now. I reply with the jokes or nonsense that still makes her laugh. So we are still part of each other."[29] And lest we think that Bayley's actions are purely spontaneous and impossibly generous, he empha-sizes Iris Murdoch's generosity to her own friends and loved ones. "I have never met anyone less naturally critical or censorious. Her own private judgements—if they were ever made—remained her own and were never voiced publicly."[30] This is, of course, another form of gene-rosity on Bayley's part, since he wants to show how his devotion to Iris during the course of her Alzheimer's was nothing heroic or special when compared to her own generosity in sharing her life with him. She was, he says, a profoundly good person, and whatever care she received was only her due.

Every different example of caring has its own trajectory, and all the different kinds of caring have their own peculiar structure. We might say, for instance, that something like autonomy, personal well-being, and the ability to care for others are the ultimate goals of parental love, while in caring for those who have AIDS or Alzheimer's, the goal is to preserve the dignity of the one who suffers while allowing her to live for as long as possible as part of the structured household. In all of these examples, there is a profound generosity in play which gives priority to the needs of the other person for the sake of her continued thriving. Noddings and others have suggested that caring is the original relationship from which the whole of ethical reflection is consequently derived. To be cared for as a child is certainly the first relationship that we experience, and it's not wrong to think that without this original form of caring we would be unable to recognize our ethical relations and responsibilities to others, regardless of who they were. As Noddings puts it, "Our relation to our children is not governed first by the ethical but by natural caring. We love not because we are required to love but because our natural relatedness gives natural birth to love. It is this love, this natural caring, that makes the ethical possible."[31] What must be emphasized, though, is the respect in which caring is also a profound expression of spiritual generosity which involves self-overcoming for the sake of others.

GENEROSITY, JUSTICE, AND LOVE

Focusing on caring as a form of generosity emphasizes the respect in which we are always dependent on others, even for our virtue or lack of it. In childhood especially, the one who cares for me is the one who can show me how to be good; for the project of virtue is not just a matter of personal effort, but one in which I can be helped or hindered by the attitudes and actions of other people. In this respect, caring for another is, perhaps, the original generosity or gift-giving virtue that helps the other person to become virtuous, or to maintain herself at the same moral level she held before the calamity of her accident or sickness. And while caring for another may be singular and unique, it is also the basis from which we may project an imaginative concern and sympathy for all of those who suffer or are ill-treated. Philosophers in the past have considered the personal domain of domestic relations—between parents and children, between friends, or between two adults in a committed relationship—as somehow less important than the larger social issues of justice. But there is good reason to rethink this hierarchy between the public and the personal, or at least, to imagine how the spiritual life developed within a particular caring relationship—such as the one between Bayley and Murdoch—could be transferred to deal with larger social issues, such as poverty, homelessness, unemployment, and crime. As Noddings points out, "Learning to care about depends on learning to care for, and that in turn depends on oneself having been cared for. . . . Instead of starting with an ideal state or Republic, we will start with an ideal home and move outward—learning first, what it means to be cared for, then to care for intimate others, and finally to care about those we cannot care for directly."[32] In this way, caring may be considered as the origin of all generosity, including its spiritual and emotional aspects.

Finally, it could be argued that mothers and fathers can't help loving their children, and so it may not be appropriate to think about caring in terms of *generosity*, but as the expression of a biological impulse that we share with most other creatures. This may be true, but the whole point is that generosity belongs to the register of life, while at the same time it is *also* a personal virtue. Generosity and love belong together, and there would definitely be something suspect in an act of generosity whose impulse was not connected to love of any kind. Such a possibility is even hard to imagine: Could we really care for someone else and generously give her our life if we had no kind of emotional attachment to her? In fact, it would not be *care*, but just an empty caretaking, if it did not involve profound attention to the reality of the other person. As we noted earlier, generous actions are those that go beyond the basic requirements of duty. They are not "called for," and it is astonishing whenever they occur. This applies to the generosity of parental care and friendship, as well as care for a partner who is stricken with Alzheimer's or AIDS. Such situations are common enough and almost routine, but the expression of generosity they embody will always remain a thing of wonder. And while such situations can be understood in terms of ethical obligation, they are also acts of love, for they create spiritual contexts of meaning, and they promote the possibility of a meaningful life. In this respect, we can now turn to forgiveness as a very concrete manifestation of spiritual generosity which *cannot* be grasped in purely rational or ethical terms.

Chapter Four

Forgiveness

Forgiveness is a spiritual possibility. It can be a completely generous act, and it seems to exceed the moral calculus that determines whether something is forbidden or required. Of course, there are situations where the *refusal* to forgive creates a new injury that replaces the original harm. Victims can also be unfairly pressured into granting forgiveness before they are ready, and while forgiveness provides healing, if it comes too soon it minimizes the offense as something that can easily be dealt with. Should we conclude that forgiveness is a personal choice that reflects one's character rather than a strictly moral consideration? Or should we insist that forgiveness follows a difficult but discernible logic that stays within the ethical domain? More to the point: In what sense is forgiveness a spiritual possibility? As we will see, forgiveness is self-overcoming, and it is a fundamental form of generosity, which can never be required. In this respect, forgiveness is *excessive* because it transcends the ordinary categories that determine our everyday life.

As we might expect from the earlier discussion of his work, Jean Améry says he could never forgive the Nazis who tortured him. He wrote that after the war he was a broken man and clung to his resentment as the only thing that allowed him to cope with his trauma. [1] Later, he responds to Simon Wiesenthal's question in *The Sunflower*—Would you forgive a dying Nazi soldier who asked you for forgiveness? Améry writes, "As I see it, the issue of forgiving or not-forgiving in such a case has only two aspects: a psychological one and a political one. Psychologically, forgiving or not-forgiving in this specific case is nothing more than a question of temperament or feeling." But then he adds, "Politically, I do not want to hear anything of forgiveness! . . . For one simple reason: what you and I went through must *not happen again, never, nowhere*. Therefore. . . I refuse any reconciliation with the criminals, and with those who only by accident did not happen to commit atrocities, and finally, all those who helped prepare the unspeakable acts with their words."[2] By limiting the discussion of forgiveness to the psychological or the political level, Améry suggests that the *ethics* of forgiveness remains an impossible question. Perhaps not surprisingly, he has no interest in the spiritual possibilities of forgiveness either. In this chapter, we must determine to what extent we *can* speak of forgiveness as a spiritual achievement and as a goal.

The issue of forgiveness is fraught with complexity, but the situation becomes more complicated still when we consider those things that are held to be *unforgivable*: the Holocaust of six million Jews and six million other undesirables, gypsies, homosexuals, and communists; the atrocities in Cambodia, Rwanda, Bosnia; the extreme violence that supported slavery in the United States or the apartheid regime in South Africa. All of this is a mountain of suffering that pushes ordinary models of forgiveness to a breaking point. In his famous sermons, published in 1726, Bishop Joseph Butler defines forgiveness as the forswearing of revenge. Butler is unclear on the precise relationship between revenge and resentment, but he claims that love and resentment are not mutually exclusive. Indeed, not to feel resentment at an injury would signify a lack of self-respect. Still, there comes a point when resentment is excessive:

> We may therefore love our enemy, and yet have resentment against him for his injurious behaviour towards us. But when this resentment entirely destroys our natural benevolence towards him, it is excessive, and becomes malice or revenge. The command to prevent its having this effect, i.e. to forgive injuries, is the same as to love our enemies; because that love is always supposed, unless destroyed by resentment.[3]

Now this is appropriate counsel for responding to personal slights and injuries. In this sermon, Butler emphasizes the spiritual well-being of the victim in dealing with her anger, especially after an apology has been made, for an apology is the reassertion of respect, which restores the precarious moral balance. Ordinarily, a heartfelt apology should be enough to elicit forgiveness, and ordinarily we should do everything in our power to maintain our natural benevolence toward others. But no words of apology, no reparation or words of atonement could even remotely address all the horrors listed at the beginning of this paragraph: The Holocaust, Cambodia, Rwanda, etc. From which it seems to follow that there *is* such a thing as a crime that cannot be forgiven, and although Butler never addresses this possibility, the ordinary logic of forgiveness appears to break down at this point.

It is often said that only the victim has the right to forgive, but one cannot ask the victims for forgiveness if they are dead. The attempt to speak for the victim could even be viewed as a new violation, and the willingness to forgive such crimes may itself be a kind of injustice that dishonors the memory of those who suffered. There are difficult questions concerning third-party forgiveness that need to be answered. But even if we limit our discussion to those who have been *personally* victimized, it is certainly the case that some people do forgive the unforgivable, and even when there is no ethical requirement to forgive, forgiveness is sometimes given as a completely generous act. All of which implies that forgiveness takes place "beyond ethics" and even beyond reason, for when forgiveness should be impossible, it can still happen—and here again, this suggests the deeper generosity of *life* which inspires self-overcoming.

In recent years, and largely in response to recent historical events, several notable thinkers have written on the problem of forgiveness: Hannah Arendt, Simone Weil, Jacques Derrida, and Julia Kristeva are among the most well-known.[4] They have different things to say, but two significant considerations seem to emerge from their work. On the one hand, the *refusal* to forgive so-called crimes against humanity is sometimes seen as a debt that we owe to the past. Forgiving is linked to forgetting, and we must never forget, and so it seems that we should never forgive. On the other hand, forgiveness is linked to the future and the possibility of healing and a new beginning, but the refusal to forgive blocks our access to an open future. Standing in the present, we find ourselves obligated both to the future and to the past: So what should be done? To forgive or not to forgive? That is the question.

The present chapter starts out from Jacques Derrida's discussion of forgiveness in two important essays, "On Forgiveness," and "To Forgive: The Unforgivable and the Imprescriptible."[5] These essays are difficult, provocative, and unsettling, and as such they mirror the difficulty and the apparent contradictions of forgiveness itself. At the same time, they offer significant insights into the nature of forgiveness, de-

spite their paradoxical claims and Derrida's admission that "there is no
theoretical statement about forgiveness. Each time I make a theoretical
statement about the event of forgiveness I am sure that I miss it."[6]
Derrida is especially open to the paradoxical nature of forgiveness, or
what he calls its *impossible* character: In what sense can we forgive the
unforgivable? Is forgiveness always *mad*? In what follows, we start
with Derrida's essays and offer a reading that illuminates underlying
spiritual themes. This discussion opens up the spiritual possibilities of
forgiveness. Then we examine the spiritual significance of forgiveness,
which is tied to the absolute generosity of life itself.

FORGIVENESS: CONDITIONAL AND UNCONDITIONAL

In his account of forgiveness, Derrida describes two very different
concepts that structure our understanding of what forgiveness is:
"Sometimes, forgiveness (given by God, or inspired by divine prescription) must be a gracious gift, without exchange and without condition;
sometimes it requires, as its minimal condition, the repentance and
transformation of the sinner . . . These two poles, *the unconditional and
the conditional*, are absolutely heterogeneous, and must remain irreducible to one another. They are nonetheless indissociable."[7] Derrida
does not name these concepts, but we could say that the conditional
pole is the rational concept of forgiveness, which also belongs to the
rational economy of the modern world. As Derrida and others have
noted, this world is organized in terms of commodification. The fact is
that today just about anything can be bought and sold, and everything
has a price, including nature, personal freedom, and human life itself.
Thinking along these lines, forgiveness can also be granted if the price
is right. This means that forgiveness is possible but it depends upon the
offender's repentance, restitution, and atonement; the goodwill of the
victim; and other factors that might be relevant. How great was the
crime? And does the offender feel enough guilt? Sometimes forgiveness will be expected—if I am late for a meeting, or even if I thought-
lessly hurt your feelings, then a sincere apology and a promise to do
better should eventually earn me forgiveness. In this situation, it makes
sense to say that I *deserve* forgiveness, and for someone to remain
angry with me would simply be wrong. It may be understandable, but
in the end it cannot be justified because this is now an obstacle to
spiritual renewal. We also need to forgive others because we know that

at some point we will need to be forgiven ourselves. Hence, this kind of forgiveness is quite reasonable, and it is the refusal to forgive that is problematic in various ways.

Sometimes, however, the offence may be too great for any apology or act of restitution that would make things right again. And at this point, we may have to say that we are dealing with something that is (rationally) unforgivable—where the other person does not deserve forgiveness, either because she has not fulfilled the conditions for forgiveness, or just because there are no conditions that could *ever* justify forgiveness from a rational point of view. Of course, Derrida has in mind the atrocity, the holocaust, or the act of murder that destroys a life and the lives of numerous others who are affected by it. He writes, "in order to approach now the very concept of forgiveness, logic and common sense agree for once with the paradox: it is necessary, it seems to me, to begin from the fact that, yes, there is the unforgivable. Is this not, in truth, the only thing to forgive? The only thing that *calls* for forgiveness?"[8] Derrida's claim, which is more than just wordplay, points to contradictions within the logic of forgiveness itself: if we only forgive what *should* be forgiven or what can be forgiven in terms of the rational concept, then we are not dealing with the most authentic and radical possibility of forgiveness, but with a kind of restitution that remains within the economy of commercial life, where I offer repentance and forgiveness is my payment. But to forgive that which is unforgivable would be the most profound expression of forgiveness that rejects this ordinary logic of exchange. Using Derrida's extreme language, it would somehow make the impossible possible, and it would exist beyond ethics and reason as a *spiritual* possibility which is more than just a *personal* accomplishment or the sign of good character.

In this way, we move to the second concept of forgiveness, which is forgiveness severed from all limiting conditions such as apology or atonement and the very words, "I forgive you," that might restore the idea of indebtedness if used to proclaim someone's superiority over someone else. The possibility of unconditional forgiveness must be understood as a pure gift, since it is not intended as an exchange for something else. It is a spiritual possibility, but since it is associated with an ideal that belongs to religion, we can also call it a *religious* concept of forgiveness because it goes beyond the secular logic of the commercial world. In the words of Jesus, during the "ultimate crime" of the crucifixion, "Father, forgive them; for they know not what they do."[9] Elsewhere in the *New Testament*, Jesus says that forgiveness should not be limited to seven times, but "seventy times seven" times, which implies that complete unconditional forgiveness is the ideal that we should always try to follow in our dealings with others.[10] Following this suggestion, John Caputo argues that Jesus may have been crucified because he taught such a doctrine of radical forgiveness, in which God forgives us even before we have repented, and even if we *never* repent of what we have done.[11] This would certainly be one way of under-standing the limitless generosity of God. Indeed, much has been written in recent years on the relationship between God and the gift, which may be a sign of the overwhelming *absence* of generosity (and the sacred) in the modern world.[12] Caputo discusses Jesus as one of the first teachers to emphasize the role of forgiveness in empowering spiritual life. In his book *On Religion*, he writes, "Jesus is not The Answer but the place of the question, of an abyss that is opened up by the life and death of a man who, by putting forgiveness before retribution, threw all human accounting into confusion, utterly confounding the stockbrokers of the finite, who always seek a balance of payments, which means who always want to settle the score."[13] Of course, there are other examples of extraordinary forgiveness in the *Old Testament*: Joseph forgives his brothers and helps them even though they had sold him into captivity years before.[14] But the imperative of forgiveness becomes explicit with Jesus. We may add that unconditional forgiveness is also "religious" insofar as it is based on radical hope in the future and the possibility of a new beginning, both for the individual and for the community itself. Indeed, such forgiveness can be an unexpected "miracle" which is transformative for all of those involved.

But what happens to the *human* standpoint in all of this? We may accept that such unconditional forgiveness is an (ideal) religious pos-sibility, but given the very limited and imperfect nature of human be-ings, it is still doubtful whether such forgiveness can ever be achieved in this life. Thus it may be the case that the concept of pure forgiveness functions as an ideal, or an absolute standard, that individual acts of forgiveness can approach but never completely achieve. And we are bound to fall short of this goal because it is hard to escape the rational economy of debt and indebtedness that seems to constrain all of our dealings with each other. Perhaps forgiveness always has a payoff—even if it is only personal gratification and feeling good about one-self—but with every payoff, forgiveness gets re-inscribed into the logic of personal exchange: it is not an absolute gift since it is done for self-regarding reasons, and this is why true forgiveness—unconditional forgiveness—is impossible. Derrida writes, "as soon as the victim 'understands' the criminal, as soon as she exchanges, speaks, agrees with him, the scene of reconciliation has commenced, and with it this ordinary forgiveness which is anything but forgiveness."[15] This does not mean that the pure concept of forgiveness is irrelevant, however, since it still functions as an inspiring ideal. And we can evaluate individual acts of forgiving as better or worse in terms of their approximation to this standard. On this reading, Derrida is not telling us that we should always forgive, he is only clarifying the concept of forgiveness.

And yet, we should also point out that such forgiveness is *possible* because sometimes the impossible happens. For example, Amy Biehl was a graduate of Stanford University who had gone to South Africa on a Fulbright scholarship. As South Africa's first all-race elections approached in 1994, she worked at Cape Town Law School to develop voter registration programs for South Africa's blacks. On August 25th, 1993, while driving some friends back to Guguletu township, her car was surrounded by a mob chanting, "one settler, one bullet." Amy was pulled from her car and killed. Her parents were devastated, but they forgave their daughter's killers and requested amnesty for them when they testified before South Africa's Truth and Reconciliation Commission. In fact, they created the Amy Biehl Foundation so that their daughter's death might lead to reduced violence in South Africa through rehabilitation programs, job skills instruction, and literacy training. Two of the men who were involved in Amy's killing even went to work at the Amy Biehl Foundation. "The logic would be that the South Africans should be giving some kind of reparation to the Biehls," said Archbishop Desmond Tutu. "They've turned it all upside down. . . . It is the victims, in the depth of their own agony and pain who say, 'the community—which produced these murderers—we want to help that community be transformed.'"[16]

A second example: In 2006, five young girls were killed by a lone gunman in the Nickel Mines Amish school shootings. A few days after this tragedy, a group of Amish, including parents of some of the girls who had been killed, visited the widow and the parents of the gunman because they knew they were also suffering intense emotional pain, and they wanted to reach out to them. The authors of a recent book on the Amish school shootings comment: "The Amish . . . led with their forgiving side, and began the struggle to make sense of their pain by extending grace. Relying on deeply engrained habits of forgiveness, they extended compassion right away, within hours of the shooting."[17] Of course, these are remarkable individuals with incredible spiritual resources, but this case is by no means unique, and there are many other examples like it that we could discuss. Here, the important point is that members of the Amish community valued forgiveness so highly they could not even think about responding in any other way.

The example of the Amish school shootings suggests that forgiveness can be fostered by the community one belongs to. We can hardly imagine a society that could continue to exist without the possibility of forgiveness, for this is what restores the community after it has been broken. Perhaps the ancient Greeks did not always think of forgiveness as a virtue—Aristotle complains about the *mild* man (the very opposite of the belligerent man) who is far too ready to forgive those who injure him. And clearly, in our own society, forgiveness is sometimes considered a weakness. People who forgive those who hurt their loved ones can be made to feel that they don't really care about their loved ones at all. But with Christianity, Buddhism, and other religious perspectives, forgiveness is more highly esteemed; at the very least, Christians and Buddhists pay lip service to the value of forgiving. Hence, there is nothing *inevitable* about the way in which we respond to deliberate harm; the value of forgiveness is to some extent culturally determined, and this means that forgiveness can be learned and cultivated as a goal, along with compassion and other positive responses.

To give one more example from a different cultural context, in *Ethics for the New Millennium*, the Dalai Lama describes the suffering and death of millions of his people since the Chinese invasion of Tibet in 1950. Among those tortured was Lopon-la, who refused to hold any grudges against those who harmed him. In fact, he deliberately cultivated compassion for his tormentors. The Dalai Lama describes his meeting with Lopon-la after the latter had been released from prison:

> More than 20 years after last seeing him, I found Lopon-la much as I remembered him. He looked older, of course, but physically he was unscathed, and mentally his ordeal had not affected him adversely at all. His gentleness and serenity remained. From our conversation, I learned that he had, nevertheless, endured grievous treatment during those long years of imprisonment. In common with all others, he had been subjected to "re-education," during which he had been forced to denounce his religion, and, on many occasions, he was tortured as well. When I asked him whether he had ever been afraid, he admitted that there was

one thing that had scared him: the possibility that he might lose compassion and concern for his jailers. [18]

This is an astonishing passage because it challenges accepted ideas about the difficulty of forgiveness and the inevitability of resentment. It suggests that true forgiveness is a spiritual achievement and not a form of weakness or self-deception. And it offers an interesting counterpoint to Jean Améry's refusal to contemplate forgiveness under any circumstances. Is such forgiveness *reasonable*? Many would say that it is *not*. In fact, Derrida frequently calls it *mad* because it requires relinquishing all claims and rejecting all the rules of equivalence that structure modern life. "Just forget it!" we say, and at that moment we seem to give ourselves away.

In an essay that appears to parallel Derrida's own work, the philosopher Berel Lang looks at Jewish perspectives on forgiveness in light of the Holocaust. In this essay, Lang describes two views of forgiveness which are not dissimilar to Derrida's own: the first in which forgiveness has to be asked for, and only the person, or the group, that has been harmed can grant it if they want to; the second, in which forgiveness is given without being asked for, without acknowledgment of wrongdoing on the part of the offender, and where forgiveness is granted by someone who was not the person wronged. Lang comments on these two concepts of forgiveness, which on the face of it are quite similar to Derrida's own:

> These two views differ so fundamentally that I do not see a way either of reconciling them or of finding a third alternative that could mediate between them: if you hold the first, you cannot hold the other; if you hold the second, you cannot hold the first. Their differences, moreover, are substantive, not semantic, certainly more than a proprietary quarrel over the term *forgiveness*: each of them leads to (and originates from) a context in which forgiveness reflects something of its common usage. [19]

Lang proposes an either/or disjunction. For Derrida, on the other hand, the rational and the "religious" concepts of forgiveness that we have described—or forgiveness in its conditional and unconditional forms—are not just two alternatives that we have to choose from. In fact, the conditional and unconditional aspects of forgiveness seem to imply and evoke each other. They are inseparable and indissociable, antagonistic and yet completely bound up together. And he notes, "I remain 'torn' (between a 'hyperbolic' ethical vision of forgiveness, pure forgiveness,

and the reality of a society at work in pragmatic processes of reconciliation). But without power, desire, or need to decide. The two poles are
irreducible to one another, certainly, but they remain indissociable."[20]
For example, politics views forgiveness as a means to reconciliation.
The Truth and Reconciliation Commission in South Africa is an obvious case in point. The professed goal of this commission is national
unity, and it offers an amnesty for those who confess their crimes. But
amnesty implies *amnesia* and forgetting and the decision not to talk
about past wrongs, and it is only a limited kind of forgiveness. Under
previous amnesties, such as the one declared in post-war France, it was
a crime to publicize the wartime wrongdoing of others, which had to be
"forgotten" for reasons of state.[21] But at the same time, behind such
practical considerations there stands a more radical concept of (unconditional) forgiveness which continues to inspire the reconciliation process, by holding out the possibility of a completely open future.

Thus, in opposition to Lang, perhaps one way of bringing the two
concepts of forgiveness together is to think of them as two different
stages in the *process* of forgiveness. The immediate forgiveness of
great wrongs is difficult if not impossible, for everything profound
takes time. But after some time has passed, the victim may begin to feel
compassion for the one who harmed him, especially if he (the victim)
accepts certain fundamental truths that apply to most human beings or
which seem to be a part of the human condition. In writing about the
troubles in Northern Ireland, for example, Nigel Biggar lists some of
these truths, including

> The truth that she herself [the victim] is no stranger to the psychic
> powers that drive human beings to abuse each other; the truth that some
> individuals, for reasons that remain hidden in the mysterious interpene-
> tration of history and the human will, are less well-equipped than others
> to resist common pressures; the truth that some are fated to find them-
> selves trapped in situations where only an extraordinary moral heroism
> could save them from doing terrible evil.[22]

None of us chose the circumstances of our birth or how we were raised
by others. There is a lot of luck here, and a lot of *moral luck*, for we
cannot always know how we would respond if we found ourselves
trapped in desperate circumstances, such as famine or war. We would
like to believe that we would always do the right thing, but our hold on
goodness may be more tenuous than we think. Our lives are shot
through with contingencies over which we have very little control, and

if we focus on this point, we are likely to feel less anger toward those who have harmed us. Some victims may also feel a strong need to rebuild relationships and restore the community that has been damaged by the harmful act, and vengeance is simply not an option for those who continue to care about the well-being of others. Hence, there may come a time when the victim is able to offer unconditional forgiveness. It is unlikely to be her first response, for typically complete forgiveness is only achieved after a long spiritual journey that includes resentment, the emergence of compassion, the overcoming of resentment, and finally, some kind of absolution for the sake of the good. Forgiveness is a spiritual process, and the "paradox" of forgiveness that Derrida describes becomes comprehensible, even possible, if we think in terms of spiritual progress *toward* unconditional forgiveness as its goal.

PARADOXES OF FORGIVENESS

We can now return to Derrida's discussion by directly addressing three of the most provocative claims that he makes about forgiveness. This will help to complete our understanding of the spiritual reality of forgiveness itself. The three claims are (1) "forgiveness forgives only the unforgivable";[23] (2) forgiveness is mad, "and it must remain a madness of the impossible";[24] and (3) forgiveness is not a modification of giving, but its "first and final truth." In Derrida's words, "Before the gift, forgiveness."[25] Derrida himself is a profoundly spiritual philosopher, and all of these paradoxical claims help to illuminate the spiritual dimension that is clarified by his writings.

First, to forgive involves forgiving the unforgivable: as we have seen, this is because forgiving the forgivable is only reasonable and even to be expected at a certain point. If I now respect you enough to apologize and make amends in some way, then I show that I esteem you, and there is no good reason not to restore the moral order, which is founded on mutual respect. The real difficulty begins when we are dealing with excessive crimes, including crimes against humanity, where the victim is usually dead and therefore unavailable to offer forgiveness. It seems that in this kind of situation, unconditional forgiveness is not only mad, but also foolish and irresponsible. In this context, for example, the philosopher Richard Bernstein argues that forgiveness should always be measured and discriminating. And he comments, "This is a *deliberative process*. And like all genuine deliberation, there is no way of avoiding the risk and gap of making responsible decisions. Without such deliberation, the very intensity, the trembling, the difficulty of forgiving the unforgivable would not make any sense."[26] From this very *reasonable* standpoint, it would be quite wrong to forgive someone who committed a terrible crime, who was not even sorry for what he did, and who never even asked for forgiveness. Several writers who respond to Simon Wiesenthal's question in *The Sunflower*—Would you forgive a dying Nazi who asked you for forgiveness?—are simply appalled that the possibility of forgiveness could even be considered in such a context. Moshe Bejski writes, "Even if Wiesenthal believed that he was empowered to grant a pardon in the name of the murdered masses, such an act of mercy would have been a kind of betrayal and repudiation of the memory of millions of innocent victims who were unjustly murdered, among them, the members of his family."[27] And Cynthia Ozick is even more insistent: "forgiveness is pitiless. It forgets the victim. It negates the right of the victim to his own life. It blurs over suffering and death. It drowns the past. It cultivates sensitiveness toward the murderer at the price of insensitiveness toward the victim."[28] Such a position is reasonable, and it may even be ethically correct, or at least morally acceptable, but it is oblivious to forgiveness as a spiritual possibility that expresses the total generosity of life.

The very idea of unconditional forgiveness seems absurd and impossible, and yet, as we have noted, it does happen. It is an act of complete generosity which is not just the product of calculation, or in spite of what Bernstein says, deliberation or *phronesis*. The latter involves weighing up all the various conditions and factors—including the extent of repentance and atonement—in order to make a well-considered decision on whether forgiveness is to be granted or not. Sometimes this happens, but in other cases, forgiveness is given even *before* repentance and atonement are offered. How can we make sense of such extraordinary examples? Take the case of Gordon Wilson: While his daughter, Marie, lay dying after a bombing in Northern Ireland, Wilson held her hand and made a decision then and there to forgive the bombers. He prayed for them, and later in an interview he begged people not to take revenge for her death because that would only make matters worse. Until the end of his life, Wilson worked hard to bring peace to the people of Northern Ireland, and this was his legacy to his daughter. In their essay on unconditional forgiveness, Garrard and McNaughton comment on this exceptional case: "Such forgiveness is clearly not conditional on any change of heart in the wrongdoer. Wilson did not wait to see if the bombers would feel remorse or change their ways. Assuming the forgiveness was genuine and that he had no ulterior motives for expressing it, it might seem churlish not to feel unreserved admiration for what he did."[29] Wilson's response can be criticized as thoughtless or even unethical (and he received many letters to that effect). It may reflect a bad policy because it seems to condone bad acts with the promise of immediate forgiveness. Many would say it shows a lack of self-respect. Aristotle might say that if someone harms you or your nearest and dearest, you *should* feel anger and indignation, and to forgive them at once is a contemptible response which shows how *weak* you are. And yet, such forgiveness does happen, and when it happens, it is an act of spiritual and emotional generosity that inspires many of those who are involved. For this is what it is to *forgive the unforgivable*.

Derrida refers to this unconditional concept of forgiveness as "mad" because it seems to escape the underlying *economic* paradigm that structures many aspects of modern life. "If I say, as I think, that forgiveness is mad, and that it must remain a madness of the impossible, this is certainly not to exclude it or to disqualify it."[30] Thinking of forgiveness as a kind of madness is also to treat it as an exceptional event, or even as an aberration; it is to show how detached it is from all the norms of the community, and how it is (apparently) a pure act of will that is not limited by conditions or even by "sufficient" reasons. Such forgiveness is an expression of the individual as an individual—uncoded, unexpected, and radically free. It avoids the spirit of violence and recrimination that usually confines us, especially when we have been hurt. But although such forgiveness is a singular expression of the individual, it is at the same time an act which is directed toward the other person rather than oneself. It is not an act that manipulates the other (even though the self has already suffered because of the other). And it is not an act that directly promotes the interests of the forgiver (which could include revenge and further violence). In forgiveness, I recognize the other person, the one who has harmed me, as a subject who is worthy of respect. But this is not exactly a good *bargain*. From the rational perspective, giving away one's claim upon the other is a kind of madness, but as a fundamental form of generosity, it is also an opening onto the sacred dimension of life, which resists all calculation and the keeping of accounts.

Seeing the other *as* an other and not manipulating her as a means to an end is the foundational act of human society. It implies the mutual respect that must exist for as long as society is to be more than just a collection of separate individuals. And in this regard, forgiveness restores the community when it has been damaged. Hence, Derrida's claim that forgiveness—radical, unconditional forgiveness—*precedes the gift*, for the latter presupposes the mutual regard of self and other which forgiveness restores:

> We must ask ourselves, breaking the symmetry or the analogy between gift and forgiveness, if the urgency of an im-possible forgiveness is not first what the enduring and non-conscious experience of the im-possible gives to be forgiven, as if forgiveness, far from being a modification or a secondary complication or a complication that arises out of the gift, were in truth its first and final truth. Forgiveness as the impossible truth of the impossible gift. Before the gift, forgiveness. Before this impossible, and as the impossible of this latter im-possible, the other. [31]

This is a difficult passage, but it is significant, and we can consider one possible way of reading it here: Derrida argues that forgiveness is the most original act of generosity. It is the gift of time that is contained in the possibility of a new beginning. Giving presupposes mutual respect between self and other, but *for-giving* (literally, "before the gift") acknowledges the other—in this case, the offender—as someone who is worthy of respect, even though the offender has already undermined respect for others by harming them. Hence, without forgiveness, the mutual reciprocity and respect that society requires would cease to exist. In a commentary on Derrida, Niva Arav puts this point more succinctly: "As the unforgivable is erasing the Other, forgiving the unforgivable means bringing back the Other that has disappeared in the unforgivable act." [32] Forgiveness is complete generosity which involves self-overcoming for the sake of the other person. It restores the society that had been damaged, and without such forgiveness no society could possibly sustain itself for long.

What Derrida grasps in his discussion of forgiveness is the extreme generosity of unconditional forgiveness and its power to liberate human lives. Forgiveness is profoundly transformative, and while there are issues concerning when forgiveness is morally permissible or required, and who has the right to forgive on any given occasion, forgiveness is in a strong sense spiritually empowering. And it is to this aspect of forgiveness that we must now direct our thinking.

FORGIVENESS AND SPIRITUAL LIFE

We have seen that unconditional forgiveness is exceptional. It is "extraordinary" and even "impossible" and seems to interrupt the unfolding of time itself: "Forgiveness is not, it *should not be*, normal, normative, normalizing. It *should* remain exceptional and extraordinary, in the face of the impossible: as if it interrupted the ordinary course of historical temporality."[33] This last comment is enigmatic, but one way of understanding this claim, that forgiveness somehow interrupts the ordinary course of historical temporality, can be found in the work of Hannah Arendt, who Derrida refers to several times in his own writings on forgiveness. In *The Human Condition*, Arendt describes forgiveness as the only possibility of renewal. She claims that without forgiveness, we would remain within the "relentless automatism of the action process," and be locked forever in the cycle of injury, anger, vengeance, and retribution.[34] But against this, forgiveness is the absolutely unexpected and incalculable response that begins the world anew. Once again, it is "the gift of time." As Arendt puts it, "forgiving, in other words, is the only reaction which does not merely re-act but acts anew and unexpectedly, unconditioned by the act which provoked it and therefore freeing from its consequences both the one who forgives and the one who is forgiven."[35] This is an important point: forgiveness confers freedom on those who are forgiven by loosening the grip of the past. And now the offender's identity is no longer constituted by her previous action, she is free to act in a more independent way, and she can reconsider the meaning of the past: "I did such a terrible thing," can become, "I have a chance to improve my life and to help others live the right way." But forgiveness also confers freedom on the one who forgives: the one who has suffered the injury of another is forced to think of herself as a victim, and is often stuck in a prison house of anger and resentment. In this respect, to forgive someone is to retake control of one's life by initiating an act that defines one as the co-creator of one's world. Such forgiveness would appear to be difficult or even impossible from an ordinary point of view. But the fact that it happens, even routinely, suggests that it comes from a standpoint that is *beyond* the ego and its selfish concerns.

Bishop Butler and other writers have noted that by confronting our rage we can often go beyond it. Forgiveness dissipates anger and returns us to a much stronger sense of our own agency. And yet, it would not be correct to think of forgiveness as primarily a selfish or even a self-oriented act. Some popular titles on forgiveness, including the bestseller by Richard Enright, *Forgiveness Is a Choice*, seem to emphasize the spiritual and emotional benefits that the forgiver will gain by "letting things go" and forgiving the person who has harmed him. Enright writes that the purpose of his book is to benefit the forgiver. For, "if you are willing to use the forgiveness process, I believe that you may be able to find freedom from anger, resentment, bitterness, and the self-destructive behavior patterns that accompany them. You may have inherited a family tradition of anger and bitterness, but you don't have to pass it on to your children and grandchildren."[36] Of course, there is a lot to be said for transcending one's rage and not remaining in a state of hostile resentment. But we can only grasp the higher possibilities of forgiveness once we go beyond the idea that forgiveness is a strategy, or something that is simply useful in achieving a particular goal, whether this is for the victim or for the offender.

As we have seen, Derrida notes that there is even something problematic about using words to express my decision to forgive. If I proclaim my forgiveness—"I forgive you"—then perhaps I am re-asserting myself as the "sovereign" subject, and turning the tables on the one who objectified me as a victim. I say that the other has been forgiven, but in this case the very act of forgiveness is used to confirm the secondary status of the other person. In what sense is this true forgiveness? As Derrida concludes his essay:

> What I dream of, what I try to think as the 'purity' of a forgiveness worthy of its name, would be a forgiveness without power: *unconditional but without sovereignty*. The most difficult task, at once necessary and apparently impossible, would be to dissociate *unconditionality* and *sovereignty*. Will that be done one day? It is not around the corner, as is said. But since the hypothesis of this unpresentable task announces itself, be it as a dream of thought, this madness is perhaps not so mad.[37]

But perhaps we should not say that the decision to forgive is an act of *sovereignty*, or a free choice of the will, since it is the process of forgiving someone else which leads to sovereignty. Forgiveness is the first step in reclaiming one's life, and paradoxically, it requires self-overcoming or letting go of oneself in order to get there. But in this respect, Derrida's "most difficult task" may actually be more achievable than he thinks.

In short, a better way of thinking about forgiveness is to see it in terms of self-overcoming, as opposed to self-assertion, and as something which typically happens over an extended period of time. This is why people who write about their own efforts of forgiveness often emphasize their sense of transcending narrow limitations and encountering a deeper spiritual reality after they found it possible to forgive. Resentment tends to isolate the victim. Overcoming resentment may not be a moral requirement, and it may not even be the most *useful* step, but it often leads to a sense of freedom and self-enlargement. For example, in *Forgiveness: A Philosophical Exploration*, Charles Griswold uses the testimony of Eric Lomax to think about the extraordinary transformative power involved in forgiving those who have hurt you.[38] Lomax was a British soldier in World War II who had been captured and tortured by the Japanese. For many years he was full of hatred and focused his resentment on the Japanese interpreter who had been in charge of his interrogation sessions. Years later, after traveling to Japan and meeting with the interpreter, who was remorseful, Lomax was able to forgive, and in his own book, *The Railway Man*, he describes his change of heart:

> As the plane tilted us over the bay of Osaka, I held my wife's hand. I felt that I had accomplished more than I could ever have dreamed of. Meeting Nagase has turned him from a hated enemy, with whom friendship would have been unthinkable, into a blood-brother. If I'd never been able to put a name to the face of one of the men who had harmed me, and never discovered that behind that face there was also a damaged life, the nightmares would always have come from a past without meaning. And I had proved for myself that remembering is not enough, if it simply hardens hate.[39]

Once the humanity of the offender became apparent—Mr. Nagase was now an elderly man like himself—Lomax was able to abandon his negative thoughts and embrace a positive and more compassionate way of being in the world. It was a spiritual turning point: once he forgave Nagase, he began to achieve wisdom and a new meaning in his life; whereas before he had always thought of himself as a victim, through this new experience of self-enlargement and spiritual growth he was able to relate to himself as the one in charge of his own life.

Sometimes the power of forgiveness is extraordinary and accomplishes a lot of good in the world. As we have seen, the parents of Amy Biehl had every reason to live in bitterness after the brutal murder of their daughter. But by forgiving her killers, and establishing the Amy Biehl Foundation, the Biehls continued their daughter's work and gave meaning to her life and her death. Similarly, by confronting his rage, Eric Lomax confronted his own potential for harm and evil, perhaps the same feelings that possessed those who committed the original violence against him. It is a common spiritual experience, and certainly one that is highlighted in Buddhism and other faiths: once we perceive the underlying suffering that pervades all life, we begin to experience a sense of connection to all others and ultimately a deep compassion for all living beings. And in this way, forgiveness is tied to compassion, the end of self-absorption, and a better sense of our own place in the basic order of things.

In this way also, forgiveness must be viewed as one of the most exceptional forms of generosity: forgiveness is a gift to the other, a willingness to give her a second chance; it is a gift to the world insofar as it ends the cycle of anger and resentment and restores the community that had been damaged; it is also a gift to oneself in which all claims are abandoned and our agency is restored. But it is not just an *ethical* achievement, for forgiveness expresses the ongoing process of spiritual transformation which involves self-overcoming leading to further en-lightenment.

Chapter Five

Reverence

At some point, we may become profoundly aware of the deeper realities that surround us, and more self-conscious of our own spiritual life. Kant, for example, says that two things are capable of inspiring him: the starry sky above him and the moral law within, for when he contemplates the immensity of the cosmos and the absolute necessity of duty, he is profoundly affected at the deepest level of his being. The experience that Kant describes belongs to the third, reflective level of spirituality, which is epitomized by the attitude of *reverence*. Reverence goes beyond the recollection of the self in suffering and the overcoming of the self in generosity. It lies halfway between worship and respect: on the one hand, worship implies self-denial in the face of something or someone like God who is completely superior and transcendent. On the other hand, respect implies equality and an agreement not to interfere in another person's life so long as she conforms to the rules of the social contract. With reverence, we acknowledge the reality of something that is greater than we are, and completely separate from our own projects and plans. But we also experience a sense of belonging by identifying with something that inspires us with joy. Reverence is often understood in a specifically religious context where it describes the self-restraint of the believer as he approaches his god. But reverence is not a specifically religious attitude because it can be associated with other objects such as truth, justice, nature, and the principle of life itself. We may have reverence for religious rituals and ceremonies; but we can also feel reverence for art and nature or humankind in general.

According to Kant, the immensity of the cosmos and the imperative force of the moral law must inspire complete devotion and reverence whenever we contemplate these things. But we are not shattered by this kind of experience; in fact, we are inspired by it, for it opens up our spiritual life in a very dramatic way. In an important passage, Kant meditates with wonder upon the origin of the moral commandment, and he expresses his reverence for duty, which constrains him, even though he cannot live up to all of its strict requirements:

> Duty! Thou sublime and mighty name that dost embrace nothing charming or insinuating but requirest submission and yet seekest not to move the will by threatening aught that would arouse natural aversion or terror, but only holdest forth a law which of itself finds entrance into the mind and yet gains reluctant reverence (though not always obedience)—a law before which all inclinations are dumb even though they secretly work against it: what origin is there worthy of thee, and where is to be found the root of thy noble descent . . . and from which to be descended is the indispensable condition of the only worth which men can give themselves?

To which he replies, "It cannot be less than something which elevates man above himself as a part of the world of sense, something which connects him with an order of things which only the understanding can think and which has under it the entire world of sense."[1] This is heartfelt and more than just an intellectual reflection. For Kant, the moral law is overwhelming, especially when we contrast its absolute necessity and power to our own limited existence: killing is wrong regardless of where or when we live; respect for others is an undeniable good; and we cannot just decide for ourselves what is right and what is wrong. But at the same time, we *belong* to the moral law because we are moral beings and moral commandments are an expression of our own higher nature. And so our connection to the moral law inspires self-respect. As Kant comments,

> But from our capacity for internal lawgiving and from the (natural) man feeling himself compelled to revere the (moral) man within his own person, at the same time there comes *exaltation* and the highest self-esteem, the feeling of his inner worth (*valor*), in terms of which he is above any price (*pretium*) and possesses an inalienable dignity (*dignitas interna*), which instills in him respect for himself (*reverentia*).[2]

To experience reverence for something—such as the moral law—is not to be diminished but ultimately uplifted by it, and we come away from this kind of experience with a strong sense of our inner worth and a profound connection to the rest of existence.

Likewise, when Kant contemplates the immensity of nature or the power of nature, in a waterfall or a storm at sea, he is overwhelmed and dwells on the physical threat that such things represent. But assuming that we are completely safe, he points out that such an experience is uplifting and inspiring once we realize that we transcend the ordinary realm of sense and as moral beings we possess a value that has no equivalent within the material world. In his *Critique of Judgement*, Kant describes this experience of nature in terms of the *sublime*, which includes such things as high mountains, volcanoes, and the limitless sea:

> Bold, overhanging, and as it were, threatening rocks, thunderclouds piled up the vault of heaven, borne along with flashes and peals, volcanoes in all their violence of destruction, hurricanes leaving desolation in their track, the boundless ocean rising with rebellious force, the high waterfall of some mighty river, and the like, make our power of resistance of trifling moment in comparison with their might.

But then he adds,

> provided our position is secure, their aspect is all the more attractive for its fearfulness; and we readily call these objects sublime, because they raise the forces of the soul above the height of vulgar commonplace, and discover within us a power of resistance of quite another kind, which gives us courage to be able to measure ourselves against the seeming omnipotence of nature.[3]

Now, we may or may not agree with Kant's analysis of this sort of experience. The important point is that the experience of the sublime is an affirmative one. It does not leave the individual crushed and despairing, but strengthened because now she is more aware of the meaningfulness of her life through opposition to that which appears to overwhelm it. The experience of the sublime is typically a very lucid and thoughtful experience, and through it the individual is spiritually enlarged as she becomes profoundly aware of her relationship to everything "outside" of her, or to everything that is. She does not experience herself as a subject who projects her interests and categories onto the world, but paradoxically enough, as an object who is addressed and even overwhelmed by something which lies beyond the circle of her own concerns.

In both of Kant's examples—the moral law and the sublimity of nature—we experience reverence for something that is much greater than we are, and something that belongs to a deeper level of reality than we typically experience in our everyday lives. In fact, the possibility of reverence shows that there are some things that we value for no other reason than the value that they have in themselves. In the same way, Plato talks about the transcendent Forms of justice, courage, temperance, and the Good. According to Plato, the Forms exist beyond space and time, and both humans and gods revere them. But they are not *useful* in any practical sense, and they don't belong to the everyday world in which everything seems to have a price. This is why we are troubled by people who are *only* concerned about making money or enhancing their own physical comfort, for such people have no sense of the profound spiritual realities that are given to us. And if they disdain things which should be revered—such as life, nature, justice, or the truth—then we regard them as spiritually limited because they cannot see anything beyond the horizon of material life, or anything much greater than themselves.

In the rest of this chapter, we consider the basic sense and significance of reverence as a spiritual possibility, and we shall examine two different examples of reverence that are closely related to each other. We shall focus on the idea of *reverence for human beings*, since this is something that is frequently overlooked—but as Karen Armstrong notes, this is a mistake, for "When people are treated with reverence they become conscious of their own sacred worth, and ordinary actions, such as eating or drinking, are lifted to a higher level and invested with holiness."[4] In Kant's philosophy, respect and reverence exist at a fairly abstract level as underlying principles associated with morality. But more recently, other thinkers have tried to clarify the nature of the I-You (or I-Thou) relationship as a positive experience of the sacred which cannot be reduced to "respect" for something else. In particular, Martin Buber's work in *I and Thou* clarifies the possibility of a spiritual encounter with another person, which seems to be characterized by the reverence that lies at the core of all meaningful human relationships. Similarly, there is also a sense of reverence for humanity or humankind in general, and given recent developments in biotechnology and artificial intelligence—such as cloning, the mapping of the genome, or the

future possibility of cyborgs, etc.—we must ask how we should understand the idea of reverence for human life, which goes beyond the
experience of reverence for any particular person. Is "reverence for
humankind" an outmoded spiritual ideal that belongs to an earlier tradition of humanism, or is it an important spiritual possibility that it would
be disastrous to lose? By looking at how the contemporary philosopher
Jean-Francois Lyotard has thought through such issues, we can finally
show how philosophy itself can become a form of reverence and a
spiritual path of inquiry.

THE MEANING OF REVERENCE

Reverence is a self-conscious spiritual attitude. But it is not defined by
any particular object such as religion, and it does not presuppose any
set of beliefs apart from the basic trust that there are important things
that we should care about and stand in awe of. In a recent book, Paul
Woodruff defines reverence as "the well-developed capacity to have
feelings of awe, respect and shame when these are the right feelings to
have."[5] This much seems correct, for awe, respect, and shame are all
self-conscious attitudes in which we acknowledge the superior reality
of something and measure ourselves against it. For example, reverence
for the moral law is presupposed in the experience of shame or regret
for not telling the truth or doing the right thing. Reverence for nature is
presupposed in the experience of awe when we encounter the beauty
and diversity of the natural world. Reverence for humankind is presupposed in the feeling of respect for other human beings, for without any
sense of reverence for the human species, we would only care about the
rights and needs of others if it was in our own best interest to do so.
Indeed, caring about strangers who suffer in natural disasters or man-
made catastrophes would be practically inexplicable if respect was just
the same thing as tolerance, or a prudential consideration which was
not ultimately founded on our *reverence* for humankind.

A precise definition of reverence is probably not possible (or even
desirable), but at this point I think we can at least say that in reverence I
have a strong sense of something that is greater than I am. It is something that makes me keenly aware of my own limitations, but I also
recognize it as an important value that I am bound to submit to. Because it is not subject to my will, this value cannot be completely
understood, and so it must include an element of mystery. Reverence is

most commonly offered up to God, but scientists and scholars may feel a similar devotion to the truth. Wordsworth, Coleridge, and other Romantic poets felt a reverence for nature; Albert Schweitzer based his ethics on the principle of reverence for life; and others have devoted themselves to "humanity" as something that must be cared for and revered. The affective dimension of reverence is crucial. Whenever I encounter something that surpasses and overwhelms me, without endangering me, I experience awe and wonder, a profound humility and a sense of my own dependence that emerges by comparison; in this situation, arrogance or indifference are completely impossible. But I am uplifted by this encounter when I recognize that I am in relationship to something which is exalted and important. Reverence therefore includes two very different kinds of emotional response that are bound together—one in which I become aware of my own insignificance, and the other in which I feel exalted with a sense of belonging to something that is profoundly meaningful. Reverence also involves a commitment to action, for I feel bound to follow and protect whatever I revere, even if sometimes this might be at the cost of my own personal comfort or even my life. Thus Socrates felt called to philosophy as the love of truth, and he told the jury at his trial that he could never give it up even if it meant suffering the death penalty: "The truth of the matter is this, gentlemen. Where a man has once taken up his stand, either because it seems best to him or in obedience to his orders, there I believe he is bound to remain and face the danger, taking no account of death or anything else before dishonor."[6]

Finally, to have reverence for nature, art, or some higher truth is to be mindful of their benefits and to follow all the proper rituals and conventions, which might include being quiet at a musical performance or behaving appropriately at a religious ceremony or a funeral— not as a kind of mechanical observance, but in thoughtful reflection upon these things. It means sharing a sense of community with those who revere the same ideal, and from this fellow-feeling we will gain respect for those we are involved with. Reverence is a spiritual attitude that involves self-conscious restraint before an ideal object, but it is also expressed in the public realm of human interaction as proper comportment toward those ideals. Thus a teacher and a student must respect each other insofar as they are both genuinely involved in the goal of learning. As Woodruff puts it, "A teacher should not treat students as equals in all things; teachers know things students do not. Still, at every level in the ladder of learning there are human beings perched with astonishing—but limited—powers of understanding and creativity. Obviously they are unequal in attainments; that is why they need to be reminded of the equality they have in reverence for the truth."[7] But if I don't do what I am called to do in such a context—if I cheat on a test, or if I am disrespectful to my teacher or to my students as fellow seekers—then I may experience a feeling of shame. For this follows from the recognition that the valued ideal—truth, justice, or humankind, etc.—has a hold on me, and I am subject to it.

RESPECT AND REVERENCE FOR OTHERS

We can now think about the possibility of reverence in the context of human relations, or reverence for other people. This is a difficult theme to articulate, but presumably it is what Confucius had in mind when he says that in being with another person—even a stranger—we should try to conduct ourselves as if we were in the presence of an important guest: "When abroad behave as though you were receiving an important guest. When employing the services of the common people behave as though you were officiating at an important sacrifice. Do not impose on others what you yourself do not desire."[8] This idea of reverence suggests that there is a sacred dimension to human interactions, and this is a spiritual reality which has to be affirmed. But how are we to understand this? Kant thinks in terms of *respect*. In *The Metaphysics of Morals*, he argues that human beings are ends in themselves. They are not objects created or endowed with a particular purpose, or things to be used by others, but autonomous subjects of their own lives, and so they possess the absolute worth of *dignity*. For Kant, everything else in the world has a price or an exchange value, but human beings are valuable in themselves. Indeed, they are literally priceless, and so they command respect as beings that must be held in high esteem, regardless of our affection for them. They must never be abused or disregarded.[9]

Kant argues that all moral agents, by virtue of their reason, can be regarded as authors of the moral law. In fact, the moral law is itself the expression of our rational nature and so we are bound to respect it and feel its authority over us. But from this he concludes that respect for other people is a *negative* duty, and reverence for other people is actually reverence for the moral law within them:

> I am not bound to revere others (regarded merely as men) that is, to show them positive high esteem. The only reverence to which I am

bound by nature is reverence for law as such (*revere legem*); and to
revere the law, but not to revere other men in general (*reverentia adver-*
sus hominem) or to perform some act of reverence for them, is man's
universal and unconditional duty toward others, which each of them can
require as the respect originally owed others (*observantia debita*).[10]

According to Kant, I am profoundly affected by the moral law, and this
leads me to respect myself and others as moral beings. Now Kant may
not have intended it in this way, but respect for others is thereby pre-
sented as something derived or secondary, rather than an original giv-
en. And this is problematic, because it suggests that in every case
principles are more important than persons. He says that we have a
strict obligation to uphold the moral law regardless of consequences
and regardless of who is involved, whether they are friends or enemies,
loved ones or strangers, but this gives us very little space for moral
negotiation, or for making decisions derived more directly from the
love and compassion that we feel for another person. In Kant, respect
for persons is an indirect and mediated relationship because it is ultimately based on reverence for the moral law. But it would be possible
to think about these things from another perspective so that the object
of reverence was not some third thing, but the other person herself. For
quite apart from our reverence for the moral law, there is, as Confucius
realized, a more immediate sense of reverence for another person,
which is manifest in our everyday dealings with others.

The philosophical background for this has been prepared by several
recent thinkers, including Buber, Levinas, and Irigaray. What brings
these thinkers together, and marks a new direction for philosophy, is
their emphasis on the priority of relationship over the terms of the
relationship itself. The independent and sovereign self that I claim as
my own personal identity is to a great extent shaped and conditioned by
my involvement with other people and their responses to me. And in
this respect, reverence emerges in the space *between* two individuals
who each experience a sense of wonder at the existence of the other
who can never be grasped in terms of their own projects, and who
always exceeds the understanding as a "mystery" that can never be
revealed. In what follows, we shall focus on Martin Buber, since his
approach remains the most promising for our attempts to think about
the nature of reverence. Buber is not a systematic philosopher who has
a comprehensive vision of the world. But he is a profound thinker with
a variety of different insights that he develops in all of his writings,

including the masterpiece *I and Thou*. Some scholars have claimed that *I and Thou* is too loose, and even vague and unsupported in places, and Buber admits that it was written in a very short period of time "under the sway of an irresistible enthusiasm."[11] But at the same time, even if *I and Thou* lacks a full repertoire of supporting arguments, these are often given in Buber's other works, while Buber's attempt to think through the nature of relationship and reverence in *this* book seems to resonate with our actual experience of the world.

Buber begins *I and Thou* with an account of the basic modalities of relationship. As he puts it, there are two "basic words," or ways of comporting oneself in the world, and he calls these basic words the "I-You" and the "I-It":

> The world is twofold for man in accordance with his twofold attitude. The attitude of man is twofold in accordance with the two basic words he can speak. . . . There is no I as such but only the I of the basic word I-You and the I of the basic word I-It. When a man says I, he means one or the other. The I he means is present when he says I. And when he says You or It, the I of one or the other basic word is also present. Being I and saying I are the same. Saying I and saying one of the two basic words are the same. Whoever speaks one of the basic words enters into the word and stands in it.[12]

The I-You encounter that Buber describes involves complete openness to the other person, and it is spoken with the whole of one's being. In this modality, I do not attempt to dominate or control the other person. Neither do I assimilate him to my own world by grasping him with fixed categories of thinking that would reduce his fundamental difference to sameness: "The relation to the You is unmediated. Nothing conceptual intervenes between I and You, no prior knowledge and no imagination; and memory itself is changed as it plunges from particularity into wholeness."[13] Thus, what distinguishes the I-You encounter is simply that I allow the other person to *be*. I listen to her and I accept her as a subject in her own right. And this, as Buber comments, involves an activity that approaches passivity: "An action of the whole being must approach passivity, for it does away with all partial actions and thus with any sense of action, which always depends on limited exertions."[14] In order to experience the presence of the other person at this encounter, I must overcome all of my fixed patterns of response and expectations about the way things need to be. It is certainly much easier and more reassuring to approach the other as something like an object that does not challenge or unsettle my world in any significant way, but this would be to miss the transformative possibilities of the encounter which lead to the deepest fulfillment of personal being.

Presumably, this is why Buber uses the example of love to clarify the most authentic case of the I-You relationship. Buber insists that love is not just a matter of private, personal feelings because it exists in the *between* of self and other, as complete reciprocity of mutual regard: "Feelings dwell in man, but man dwells in his love. This is no metaphor but actuality: Love does not cling to an I, as if the You were merely its 'content' or object; it is between I and You. Whoever does not know this, know this with his being, does not know love."[15] Buber's comments here may speak more directly to romantic love, but the paradigm for the I-You relationship between human beings is something more like friendship. For in such a relationship the I does not seek to overwhelm and consume the You or abandon itself in slavish adoration of the beloved (which are sometimes features of romantic love). In friendship, the otherness of the friend is recognized as definitive and cannot be overcome without loss to the relationship itself. Hence, we are bound to take our friends seriously and to try to look at things from their point of view since their point of view is just as important and just as valid as our own. We value our friends and we want to be valued by them, and in this way we experience an enhancement of being and a sense of who we are. Moreover, the relationship between friends can be regarded as an ongoing dialogue in which the truth is not the personal possession of the one or the other but emerges from the encounter between the two of them. I am not suggesting that every I-You relationship must culminate in some kind of friendship; the I-You relationship is more like an epiphany that can suddenly arise in any encounter of everyday life. Buber's other examples, which include the teacher-pupil relationship, and even the possibility of an I-You relationship with the tree, make this apparent. But in friendship we are given an outstanding example of the I-You relationship that shows how the I of the I-You is formed through this original apprehension of the other and the world.

The second basic form of encounter that Buber describes is that of the I-It relationship in which I grasp the other person in terms of my own established categories of experience. In the I-It relationship I relate to the other as a limited being with a specific existence in space and time; I thereby encounter the other as an object that has a set position within my own horizon of thought; I remain self-contained and complete, and I am not fundamentally affected at all. As Buber comments,

"In the language of objects: everything in the world can—either before or after it becomes a thing—appear to some I as its You. But the language of objects catches only one corner of actual life."[16] The I-It relationship belongs to the same general movement of domination and mastery that characterizes the modern world and the triumph of instrumental reason that we associate with modern technology. Buber does not oppose the I-It relationship, which seems to be an inevitable feature of living in the world and dealing with countless others. But he argues that something extremely important is lost when *all* human relationships are reduced to the same monotonous level. In fact, what is lost is the *spiritual* nature of human existence itself: "And in all the seriousness of truth, listen: without It a human being cannot live. But whoever lives only with that is not human."[17]

In Part Three of *I and Thou*, Buber moves into explicitly religious territory. In fact, he proclaims from the outset that the I-You always leads beyond itself to the "eternal You":

> Extended, the lines of relationships intersect in the eternal You. Every single You is a glimpse of that. Through every single You the basic word addresses the eternal You. The mediatorship of the You of all beings accounts for the fullness of our relationships to them—and for the lack of fulfillment. The innate You is actualized each time without ever being perfected. It attains perfection solely in the immediate relationship to the You that in accordance with its nature cannot become It.[18]

Now we could accept these comments as a straightforward statement of Buber's own religious faith, which implies that the only way to reach God is through human beings, or something along those lines. But whatever Buber's own religious beliefs may have been, in this passage he is certainly not suggesting that the I-You relationship is somehow proof of an independent God, for a being who is thought to exist outside of every encounter is ultimately an object—albeit the supreme object—whose relationship to us is limited. On the other hand, what Buber does suggest in this passage is how the I-You encounter puts us in touch with the sacred dimension of life itself. Here, if anywhere, "God" is revealed, and the religious metaphor serves to clarify the exalted nature of the I-You relationship and its transformative possibilities. The sacred or the holy is not elsewhere in some remote beyond, it is not something to hope for in the future, but something that is revealed in the here and now in the authentic I-You encounter with another person. This is the truly transformative encounter, and to experience it is to realize that life does not require a justification that is outside of itself. As Buber comments, the encounter gives "the inexpressible confirmation of meaning. It is guaranteed. Nothing, nothing can henceforth be meaningless. The question about the meaning of life has vanished. But if it were still there, it would not require an answer."[19] In such relationships, life reveals itself as inherently meaningful and full of spiritual possibility.

In this way, then, the I-You relationship is profoundly significant as the way in which we experience another person as the subject of her own life. And it is the continual resurgence of this possibility that inspires reverence, even when our habitual responses have apparently become fixed or routine. On the one hand, *respect* involves the calculation of our duties and responsibilities, which may be viewed as part of our objective relationship with others, and it is an important feature of the I-It world. But on the other hand, respect is empowered by reverence for another person, which is original to the I-You relationship. And this is a sacred form of encounter. It involves a deep connection to the uniqueness of the other person and a sense of the mystery of another life that will never be mine.

By describing the "I-You relationship," and evoking a sense of the other in heightened, poetical language, Buber helps us to understand the origins of respect in the awe and reverence that we can feel for another person. Against Kant, respect is secondary and presupposes reverence. And reverence does not involve self-abasement or self-abandonment, but the sense of a relationship to that which is absolutely important, even "sacred." In what follows, we show how this account of reverence can help us come to grips with the discussion of humanism and even "posthumanism," which has become more urgent given recent developments in artificial intelligence and biotechnology. Where are we going as a species? And, what does it even mean to be human anymore? By thinking through such issues and following the path of thinking that a contemporary philosopher describes, we see how philosophy itself can be the expression of reverence and spiritual understanding.

LYOTARD AND THE POSTHUMAN WORLD

When the first working draft of the human genome project was unveiled in June 2000, it evoked a huge response from scientists, ethicists, and the lay population. For some it was a cause for celebration and an incredible scientific advance that would allow the human species to control its own destiny; while for others, it was a cause for profound misgiving and suspicion since it announced our willingness to play God by manipulating life for our own selfish reasons. To map out the human genome, as many commentators argued, was to grasp in complete detail what it means to be human, at least from a biological perspective. But now that we "know" what a human being is, it also becomes possible to go beyond ourselves to create a posthuman future that in no way resembles the accidental determination of our past existence as a species. Through the manipulation of the genome, through cloning, as well as developments in robotics and artificial intelligence, we can radically redefine ourselves as a species. It seems that biology is no longer destiny, and we are now at the threshold of a new age in which we may program human life in the same way that we can genetically modify our crops to make them hardier or more resistant to disease. And this means that "human nature," if it ever existed in the first place, can no longer be regarded as a brute factum or an obstacle that cannot be overcome.

But how are we to respond to the "posthuman" future that is fast becoming our own? Should we simply reject cloning and genetic manipulation of all kinds as immoral? One response will be to say that cloning is wrong because it bypasses sex, and so it is obviously at variance with the principles of natural reproduction. But this assumes that there is such a thing as "the natural order" which must always remain the same. From this point of view, even something like an artificial heart would be morally problematic. Nietzsche wrote of a time to come, after what he called the death of god, when "all the daring of the lover of knowledge is permitted once again."[20] Perhaps the *supporters* of cloning and the new technologies will argue that we are living at just such a time and we should embrace these new developments with the sense that they expand the horizon of human possibility. But just because we *can* do it, it does not mean that we *should* do it. And our love affair with the new technology and all its dazzling possibilities may actually blind us to our moral responsibilities. Indeed, cloning introduces the possibility of new eugenics programs in which people will be bred for special capacities and talents, as masters or as slaves. Is this a future that we could possibly desire for ourselves? And is there any reason to suppose that, like other eugenics programs, it would not also terminate those individuals who are "not worth saving"?

At this point, we may consider the work of Jean-Francois Lyotard, who shows in several books and essays how philosophy can itself become a kind of reverence for the spiritual life of humankind. Lyotard's essays in his book *The Inhuman* are an attempt to think through the most basic features of contemporary life—the progressive unfolding of techno-science and rapid development of every kind, which are linked to capitalism.[21] Lyotard calls this the "inhuman," for his point is the more we are conditioned and engulfed by this movement, which creates consumers with similar desires, the more we lose any real control over our lives and our desires; in losing this personal autonomy, we are losing what humanists have always valued as the most important aspect of our humanity. In this way, we *become* the "inhuman" that has already infiltrated human existence, and we lose our sense of being *unique* individuals with a life of our own. We need to recover our spiritual life, and this can be done by focusing on what it is that makes us human in the first place. Philosophy can help us to think through these issues, and in this way it can itself become a kind of reverence that illuminates spiritual themes and so returns us to them.

In the essay "Can Thought Go On without a Body?" Lyotard speculates on whether machines may eventually be programmed to take over all human functions, with the goal of prolonging life indefinitely.[22] If this happens there would be almost limitless possibilities for the continual development of what he refers to collectively as "techno-science," or the nexus of capitalism and scientific progress. In fact, Lyotard notes, the only conceivable limit to the development of techno-science would be something like the death of the sun, which is scheduled to take place about 4.5 billion years from now. And this is the context for the question that he poses here: "Can thought go on without a body?" Underlying this question, however, the deeper issue being raised is whether the kind of thought that survives its abstraction from the human context would be anything like human thought at all. Lyotard uses this question for thinking about the possibility of posthumanism: What are the limits of artificial intelligence? And does human thought depend on some features that necessarily belong to our physical embodiment?

Perhaps in this respect, Lyotard is following in the footsteps of Descartes, who asks, in the *Discourse on Method,* whether someone could ever create a machine that was indistinguishable from a human being. Descartes denies this possibility, affirming that human beings are not reducible to their physical determination, since they are both body and mind and the latter is not just an aspect of the brain. But Descartes also comments that the relationship between the mind and the body is much closer and more intimate than the relation between a pilot and his ship, and he concludes the *Discourse on Method* by asserting the integral relationship between the two different aspects of our unitary being.[23] In his own essay, Lyotard follows Descartes's lead by developing some aspects of the intimacy that exists between thought and its corporeal ground: the mind is not contained by the body but actively conditioned by it; indeed, it is a relationship of mutual determination. If Lyotard is right, then any thinking that might be able to continue without a human body would not be *human* thinking—assuming we would want to call it "thinking" in the first place. We can now follow the spiritual meditation that Lyotard pursues, which is also an expression of *reverence.* For here, philosophy returns to its original inspiration, which is to go beyond the habitual ways of thinking about things, to discover new perspectives which unsettle the subject and open up the world.

Lyotard's essay is constructed in the form of a dialogue between He and She. He begins by reflecting on the ultimate disaster that is posed by the inevitable destruction of the sun. This is an absolute limit that we cannot think around and which spells the end of all possibility:

> Of that death alone, Epicurus ought to have said what he says about death—that I have nothing to do with it, since if it's present, I'm not and if I'm not present, it's not . . . Solar death implies an irreparably exclusive disjunction between death and thought: if there's death, then there's no thought. Negation without remainder. No self to make sense of it. Pure event. Disaster.[24]

Human thought from its most basic to its most elevated levels obviously depends upon the proper functioning of the human body, which is the "hardware" that supports the sophisticated "software" that is the life of the mind. But the human body cannot survive the death of the sun. And so, at least in principle, the task for techno-science becomes straightforward: "Manufacture hardware capable of 'nurturing' software at least as complex (or replex) as the present-day human brain, but in non-terrestrial conditions. That clearly means finding for the 'body' envisaged a 'nutrient' that owes nothing to biochemical components synthesized on the surface of the earth through the use of solar energy."[25] —All this sounds more like a science-fiction scenario or a strange conceptual puzzle that isn't obviously relevant to anything else. But the underlying point is just to think about the limits of the human and the inhuman and whether the latter could ever completely assimilate the first. And even if it was possible to overcome the technical problems posed by hardware and software, in what sense would it be human thought that survives? Given the obvious differences between the way that computers think—digitally and directedly—and how humans think—analogically and hypothetically (or some would say, with "intuition")—He concludes that the nature of human thought is finally inseparable from the human reality it belongs to.

In her response, She affirms and even deepens this conclusion by showing in more detail how human thought cannot really be separated from its corporeal basis. In particular, She dwells on three interrelated structures: perception, suffering, and gender, which condition the reality of what we know as human thinking. This is not a sustained argument that leads inexorably toward a final conclusion, but a series of reflections, or "peregrinations," that explore what is most distinctive about human thought. It is also an exploratory essay that illustrates the possibility of reverence as a philosophical virtue.

First of all, She points out that human perception is always partial and incomplete; it involves synthesizing what is apprehended from one moment to the next and recognizing objects through the unlimited variation of different possible perspectives that can be taken: "Continuing vision preserves along with it what was seen an instant before from another angle. It anticipates what will be seen shortly. These syntheses result in identifications of objects, identifications that never are completed syntheses that a subsequent sighting can always unsettle or undo."[26] But in much the same sense, *human thought* is also partial and proceeds by considering its object from different perspectives, but never reaching a final complete recognition since there are always more points of view: "In any serious discussion of analogy," She comments,

> It's this experience that is meant, this blur, this uncertainty, this faith in
> the inexhaustibility of the perceivable, and not just a mode of transfer of
> the data onto an inscription-surface not originally its own. Similarly,
> writing plunges into the field of phrases moving forward by means of

adumbrations, groping towards what it "means" and never unaware, when it stops, that it's only suspending its exploration for a moment (a moment that might last a lifetime) and that there remains, beyond the writing that has stopped, an infinity of words, phrases and meanings in a latent state, held in abeyance, with as many things "to be said" as at the beginning.[27]

The phenomenology of perception is key to understanding human thinking as well, and the one is not really separable from the other. We would add that human beings are *in* the world in a much deeper sense than just occupying particular spatial-temporal coordinates. Human beings have a sense of belonging. They are comforted and exalted by certain landscapes and locales while they are distressed by others. Their sense of place profoundly affects and animates their reflection; along with their sense of temporality, age, and uncertainty facing the future. By contrast, the computer is always outside of the data it processes. It has no sense of place, being indifferent, and is uninvolved with the data it is given. For a machine, here and now can never refer to anything except a set of spatial-temporal coordinates that are extrinsic and therefore indifferent to its overall functioning.

This leads to the second line of thinking that She develops at this point: "But," she comments, "another question bothers me. Is it really another question? Thinking and suffering overlap."[28] This is a curious thing to say, but the discussion which follows clarifies this claim and is an example of the more general point that Lyotard wants to make: Real thinking, as opposed to calculation, is always difficult and painful because it avoids the easy formulations of received ideas. Certainly, as we have seen, suffering provokes thinking—the problematic, the difficult, and the strange have always demanded a response. But the point is that thinking itself is bound up with suffering insofar as it does not accept the comfort of what has already been thought. Thus, whether or not a computer actually "thinks," its operations are all task-oriented, and it follows its own basic rules of functioning to organize, calculate, and control its material or data. It simply doesn't accept whatever resists its current ordering framework, and its goal is to assimilate difference to its own self-identical order. On the other hand, human thinking, at least when it isn't merely calculation, seems to involve an openness to the outside that allows whatever is given to approach and offer itself to thought: "Thinking, like writing or painting, is almost no more than letting a givable come towards you."[29] And, "In what we call thinking the mind isn't 'directed' but suspended. You don't give it rules. You teach it to receive. You don't clear the ground to build unobstructed: you make a little clearing where the penumbra of an almost-given will be able to enter and modify its contour."[30] This is thought as openness and readiness to receive. It is the resolution not to be resolute, not to rely on fixed determinations and received ideas, and this causes our discomfort and lack of ease. "The unthought hurts," Lyotard comments,

> because we're comfortable in what's already thought. And thinking, which is accepting this discomfort, is also, to put it bluntly, an attempt to have done with it. That's the hope sustaining all writing (painting, etc.): that at the end, things will be better. As there is no end, this hope is illusory. So: the unthought would have to make your machines uncomfortable, the uninscribed that remains to be inscribed would have to make their memory suffer.[31]

But suffering does not have a good reputation in the technological realm. Indeed, it epitomizes inefficiency and less than maximal functioning. The very idea of a well-functioning machine does not rest easy with the idea of suffering and complete openness or *vulnerability* to whatever is outside it.

Finally, there is the fact of gender, which is a fixed determination of the human condition. Bodies are gendered male and female, but this difference is also inscribed and experienced from within, and conditions thought through the mediation of desire. One person, or one gender, will never be complete in itself, for it must always experience itself as a *lack* and be driven by the desire for completion in another. The computer is self-sufficient in its neutrality, and it is safe from the distractions of desire. But in this respect, it cannot experience any drive toward transcendence and the yearning that desire represents. It is safe from such suffering, but once again, it has to be said that it is this suffering which constitutes human thinking itself. Indeed,

> To that which without gendered difference would only be a neutral experience of the space-time of perceptions and thoughts, an experience in which this feeling of incompleteness would be lacking as unhappiness . . . to this neutrality gendered difference adds the suffering of abandonment because it brings to neutrality what no field of vision, or thought can include, namely, a demand.[32]

This "demand" is the force of desire that experiences its own lack and urge for completion, which is seldom if ever given. Once again, to replicate human thought these machines would have to be partial—they would have to be gendered and suffer from their essential incompleteness.

Lyotard's meditation in *The Inhuman* is a reflective encounter with "posthumanism" that describes at least three particular differences between humans and machines—perception, suffering, and gender (or desire)—which follow from the limitations of human embodiment that shape and condition the nature of thought. For anything like *human* thought to go on without a body, these fundamental aspects of embodiment would somehow have to be re-inscribed in a different physical medium. But this suggests an impossibly self-defeating task if the ultimate goal is to create a self-sufficient thinking machine that would be impervious to the death of the sun.

Lyotard's essay testifies to the affinity between philosophy and spirituality. For in this essay, Lyotard does not rely on ordinary paths of thinking; he does not offer a traditional account of human nature (which could always be challenged), but at the same time his discussion expresses profound concern for the question concerning humanity as a question that is still to be determined. In a similar sense, Heidegger says that human beings are those for whom *existence is a question*, and the task this enjoins upon us is not to *answer* the question once and for all, but to ask the question in significant ways and so to sustain its possibility.[33] In fact, philosophy becomes a form of spiritual life whenever thinking risks itself, by illuminating new perspectives and new vistas on truth that unsettle established forms of understanding, and returns the thinker to the openness of the world. For when the philosopher puts herself in question, and accepts all the risks of thinking, she affirms the priority of the truth as a higher value than her own life. In this way, Lyotard shows us how philosophy, as thoughtful meditation, can embody the spiritual value of reverence itself.

We can now turn to joy, which is the fulfillment of spiritual life and its reflective goal.

Chapter Six

Joy

"Joy" belongs to the affective dimension of spiritual attunement, and it reflects our sense of being part of a more meaningful reality than the one that usually concerns us. It may also signify the end of a spiritual journey, a proper perspective on material life, and a sense of belonging to the truth. For in joy—as opposed to pleasure or contentment—we actively celebrate life as something that is inherently meaningful and good. With *reverence* we become aware of greater realities that command our attention and evoke self-conscious restraint. But in joy we affirm our participation in those realities which may be collectively referred to as the forms of spiritual life. Of course, these things are difficult to articulate, and we may lack the language for them because our spiritual vocabulary is so impoverished. But it would be true to say that in *tranquility, joy*, or *bliss*, we feel completely at one, or at peace, with "ultimate reality," however this is understood. This chapter clarifies the possibility of joy as a spiritual theme by looking at some experiences that thinkers—including Rousseau, Nietzsche, and the very earliest philosophers—have singled out for special attention and treatment. For in the end, joy is not just mindless exuberance, but a privileged emotion in which spiritual realities are disclosed and affirmed.

In his final work, the *Reveries of the Solitary Walker*, Jean-Jacques Rousseau describes an exceptional kind of experience that he had on the island of St. Pierre while walking, drifting in a boat, and just sitting by the shore of a lake. At this point in his meditation, Rousseau is lamenting the fact that none of our earthly joys ever lasts long and that happiness is fleeting. But even if we could experience the keenest pleasure, he asks, could we truthfully say we would ever want such a moment to last forever? Then he continues,

> But if there is a state where the soul can find a resting-place secure enough to establish itself and concentrate its entire being there, with no need to remember the past or reach into the future, where time is nothing to it, where the present runs on indefinitely but this duration goes unnoticed, with no sign of the passing of time, and no other feeling of deprivation or enjoyment, pleasure or pain, desire or fear than the simple feeling of existence, a feeling that fills our soul entirely, as long as this state lasts, we can call ourselves happy, not with the poor, incomplete and relative happiness, such as we find in the pleasures of life, but with a sufficient, complete and perfect happiness, which leaves no emptiness to be filled in the soul. [1]

This is a difficult experience to articulate, but as a novelist and a philosopher, Rousseau attempts to describe it, and he ponders its spiritual significance. For him, more than anything else it is the pure unmediated experience of being itself, unencumbered by personal desires and goals:

> What is the source of our happiness in such a state? Nothing external to us, nothing apart from ourselves and our own existence; as long as this state lasts we are self-sufficient like God. The feeling of existence, unmixed with any other emotion is in itself a precious feeling of peace and contentment, which would be enough to make this mode of being loved and cherished by anyone who could guard against all the earthly and sensual influences that are constantly distracting us from it in this life and troubling the joy it could give us. [2]

As Rousseau points out, this is not exactly a personal experience or a selfish feeling of pleasure. In fact, it is defined by the absence of personal longing. More positively, it is a disinterested feeling of joy, which exults in the existence of the world and our sense of belonging to it. Here, we experience ourselves as an integral part of the cosmos, and our joy implies a fundamental gratitude for what we have been given.

Rousseau describes this experience as one of *tranquility*, but other writers have known the same experience under different names and sought to describe it in terms of *happiness, enjoyment, nirvana,* or *bliss*. In what follows, we shall call it *joy*. This kind of joy is a global feeling which is not fixated on any particular object; it is an exalted state of being rather than just a response to something that has happened. Joy involves gratitude for life, which affirms itself through us. And since it expresses the affirmation of existence, it is also the opposite of suffering, or the affliction of being, with which this book began.

In the rest of this chapter, we shall look at three different attempts to articulate (and inspire) the experience of joy. First, the Stoics have a reputation for dourness, but Stoic well-being involves exuberant joy. The Stoics called it *gaudium* and affirmed it as a fundamental experience, even while they condemned all other emotions as *pathe*, or feelings that afflict us and which should be overcome. For the Stoics, one of the most important goals is to grasp the full reality of the present moment unclouded by the past or the future: such an authentic encounter gives us the deepest happiness and the fullest joy of which we are capable. Stoics seem to be individualists who emphasize self-control, but we may ask, how can this attitude be reconciled with the sense of complete belonging to the world that provokes the Stoic experience of joy?

As we have seen in an earlier chapter, Nietzsche was preoccupied with the problem of suffering and its relationship to a meaningful life. In his own work, he projected the possibility of radiant joy as the other side of suffering and its necessary accompaniment. Nietzsche condemned reactive emotions such as pity, but he sought to inspire the exultant affirmation of life through strategies like the eternal recurrence, or the joy of Dionysian abandon. Through the eternal recurrence, Nietzsche also affirms the absolute importance of each moment as something that can joyfully be affirmed as an end in itself. But to what extent can joy be *chosen* or affirmed by an act of will? This part of Nietzsche's doctrine is problematic, and it must be closely examined. Likewise, in opposition to Nietzsche, it isn't clear that anything and everything should be celebrated simply because it happened! Finally, returning to the very beginning of philosophy, one of the key themes of *The Upanishads* is the illusory character of the everyday self that we are so profoundly attached to. The goal of *The Upanishads* is freedom, not freedom in the sense of being able to do whatever we want, but freedom *from* the everyday self and a return to the experience of Atman, the deepest level of who we are. But Atman *is* Brahman—or the ultimate ground of things—and so it follows that we are also one with absolute reality itself. Once again, this is not just an intellectual argument, but a profound *experience* that is deeply transformative. And it is grasped as a blissful, joyful experience that brings us release (*moksha*)

from the turmoil of our everyday lives. The relationship between spirituality and joy is thereby acknowledged at the very start of philosophy,
and such joy belongs to the heart of wisdom itself. But to what extent
can the mystical insights of *The Upanishads* be supported by impartial
reason? And how should we understand this kind of philosophical poetry, which evokes an *experience* without providing a more sustained
analysis of it?

In each case—Stoicism, Nietzsche's philosophy, and the early Vedanta philosophy of India—joy is experienced as a non-selfish emotion
which reveals the world to us. This is not to say that we should trust
every feeling of joy as an authentic disclosure of the world. But there is
significant convergence on the importance of joy, which involves ecstatic self-loss and identification with ultimate spiritual realities. Joy is
overwhelming, and when it comes, it seems as if it will last forever. It
is *inside* me, but at the same time it is also experienced as something
that is *out there*, the ultimate reality of the world which is open to
spiritual inquiry. The original passage from Rousseau, quoted above,
can now be understood in the same light as a paradigmatic example of
the true experience of joy.

THE TRUTH OF JOY

In the last chapter, we examined reverence as a restrained and thoughtful attitude which emphasizes the separate nature of our own existence.
In reverence we look outside ourselves and beyond ourselves to the
most fundamental realities that support us and inspire us. Reverence is
not the same thing as worship, but it is more than respect, since it
accepts that the other—whether this is nature, truth, or God—is greater
than we are. Joy is different, because it is ecstatic rather than restrained,
and it is certainly not the same thing as pleasure, which is our ordinary
goal in life. In fact, it would be true to say that joy *comes to us*, for we
can only experience joy when we no longer try to be in control of
everything that happens. Joy is felt in the affective encounter with
authentic spiritual realities. It is an important aspect of spirituality, if
not the *culmination* of our spiritual life, for it involves the most complete identification with spiritual truth at the heart of being.

Here, we can try to articulate some of the basic aspects of joy as an
experience and a spiritual goal, although this will be difficult because
joy is not a typical emotion. Sometimes joy has an object—success,

money, or honor—which is the obvious cause of our enjoyment. But at other times, joy sweeps over us, and even if there is something that provokes our joy, it does not seem to depend on anything in particular in order to exist. Ordinary emotions, such as fear, grief, and anger, are directed toward objects that affect us in some way. Fear is always fear of something; anger is focused on someone or something that upsets us; and grief is always sadness about something that has happened, such as the death of a loved one. In many cases, joy also has its own object. When someone wins a contest or creates something exceptional, they are happy and filled with joy because of what they have achieved. The very idea of "en-joyment" presupposes an object that we delight in. But joy is an exceptional emotion because it is also possible to feel joyful about *everything* or nothing in particular. We say that we are "flooded" or filled with joy, and while such an experience may be triggered by something—the image of my child, or my beautiful surroundings—this is not simply the *object* of my joy, which may have no particular focus. At the same time, joy is not just a physical sensation; it is a pleasurable emotion, but it is also *intentional* in the sense of being an affirmation of meaning in the world. And what exactly this is—what we enjoy when we feel complete joy—must now be ascertained.

We have already considered one example of "object-less" joy in the extract from Rousseau's book, the *Reveries of the Solitary Walker*. In this passage, Rousseau describes a blissful state of being which he refers to as a "simple feeling of existence." This seems to be much deeper than ordinary happiness, which is conditioned by particular pleasures, or by the overcoming of obstacles to our own well-being. Rousseau emphasizes that this sort of joy is not a selfish feeling which involves our own advantage, since one has to overcome all personal considerations in order to experience it in the first place. But what he describes is not an ordinary emotion that would be unreflective and focused on an object; it is rather a *reflective* emotion which is focused on the experience of joy, and therefore enjoys itself. Rousseau discusses it in terms of our own "godlike" self-sufficiency, for when we have this experience it seems there is nothing that resists us, and nothing that we lack; at least for the moment, we are in complete attunement with the world, and our sense of belonging is the source of the joy that we feel.

In this way, then, joy appears to disclose the deepest character of the world to us. But it is not an active encounter with the world since it does not involve manipulation or control of any kind: we simply let things be. And it is not just a passive form of encounter either, for it is not something that happens unless we are already open and ready to receive it. As we have noted, this kind of joy is a reflective emotion. It involves serenity and excitement and a sense of being in attunement with the ultimate reality and truth that underlies our ordinary lives. And since this joy is ecstatic and affirmative, it inspires us to remain in this state of being, or to recover it whenever we can. It motivates our spiritual inquiries, and it serves as a confirmation of their reality and truth.

THE STOICS AND JOY

Rousseau says that the source of true happiness lies in "nothing external to us, nothing apart from ourselves and our own existence," and he commends this state as a form of self-sufficiency that is practically divine. In this respect, Rousseau seems to confirm the Stoic view that lasting joy can only be experienced by the one who has achieved complete personal sovereignty and self-control. For the Stoics, our emotions are *pathe*, or things that we undergo or suffer. On the face of it, we don't simply choose to be angry or excited about something that happens; these feelings happen *to* us, and they undermine our personal autonomy by making us dependent on other things. In contrast to this, the Stoics insist that we should be true to ourselves by following our own higher nature as an integral part of the cosmos. We must remain vigilant and try to overcome our passions and desires through various spiritual exercises, for in this way we can harmonize with nature itself. The (Stoic) philosopher is the model of how we should live. As Seneca puts it,

> The philosopher . . . alone knows how to live for himself: he is the one, in fact, who knows the fundamental thing, how to live. The person who has run away from the world and his fellow-men, whose exile is due to the unsuccessful outcome of his own desires, who is unable to endure the sight of others more fortunate, who has taken to some place of hiding in his alarm like a timid, inert animal, he is not living for himself, but for his belly and his sleep and his passions—in utter degradation, in other words.[3]

Of course, we cannot control what happens to us. An earthquake, a disease, or an assault by others can undermine all of our best laid plans.

But what is in our power is to live virtuously, and always choose to do the right thing. And in this way, we put ourselves in attunement with nature, or the cosmos, which is rational, divine, and good.

The wise person, the Stoic sage, is one who has achieved *ataraxia*, or peace of soul, by controlling all his passions. He accepts that only some things are up to us—our opinions, impulses, desires, and aversions—"in short, whatever is our own doing"[4] —while other things, including our bodies, possessions, and reputations, are not. In this way, he becomes autonomous and free. Meanwhile, the rest of us are often carried away by our emotions, and when we experience anger, hope, or fear, it's because we have failed to understand the real distinction between that which is up to us and that which is not. Indeed, we cling to what must be taken away from us, and we refuse to accept our natural limitations. At first glance, though, the Stoic sage, who is apparently self-contained and unaffected by others, seems to be an almost inhuman ideal, and not necessarily one that is worth striving for. He has the security of self-containment, but at the same time, he is separated from others and mostly unaffected by them; he is apparently limited to a life without affect of any kind. Hence, the image of the tranquil Stoic who is unaffected by love or death or any typical human experiences.

The interesting thing, however, is that Stoic philosophers frequently talk about the experience of joy (*gaudium*), which comes at the point that one achieves complete tranquility or *ataraxia*. And in contrast to the fleeting pleasures of the body or the mind, such joy is held to be lasting and permanent. In his twenty-third Letter, for example, Seneca tells his friend Lucilius that the most important thing is to "learn how to feel joy." And he challenges him: "Do you think that I am now robbing you of many pleasures when I try to do away with the gifts of chance, when I counsel the avoidance of hope, the sweetest thing that gladdens our hearts? Quite the contrary; I do not wish you ever to be deprived of gladness. I would have it born in your house; and it is born there, if only it be inside of you."[5] Here, Seneca makes a distinction between pleasures that are not lasting, and which for the most part are not up to us, and a deeper happiness—or joy—that we experience when we are completely at one with the cosmos itself. "Real joy," he writes, is a "stern matter," by which he means that this kind of joy is not giddy or "cheerful" in any ordinary sense. Ordinary happiness is fleeting and dependent upon other things, "but the joy of which I speak, that to which I am endeavoring to lead you, is something solid, disclosing itself the more fully as you penetrate into it."[6] Such joy can hardly be

momentary because it reflects our underlying sense of complete belonging and identification with the world.

The explicit goal of Stoicism is virtue. Indeed, "the highest good is
a mind that scorns the happenings of chance, and rejoices only in
virtue." [7] But once virtue is achieved, it inspires a kind of reflective joy
in which we approach the divinity of gods. Once again, Seneca puts it
in the most compelling way, when he asks rhetorically:

> For what prevents us from saying that the happy life is to have a mind
> that is free, lofty, fearless and steadfast—a mind that is placed beyond
> the reach of fear, beyond the reach of desire, that counts virtue the only
> good, baseness the only evil, and all else but a worthless mass of things,
> which come and go without increasing or diminishing the highest good,
> and neither subtract any part from the happy life nor add any part to it?

And he adds, "A man thus grounded must, whether he wills or not,
necessarily be attended by constant cheerfulness and a joy that is deep
and issues from within, since he finds delight in his own resources, and
desires no joys greater than his inner joys." [8] For the Stoic sage, complete happiness involves living wholly in accordance with nature, but
nature is not indifferent—it is rational and good—and so we achieve
the highest condition once we identify ourselves, through virtue, with
nature or the cosmos itself. In this respect, *joy* is the sign of spiritual
achievement in which we experience an integral sense of belonging to
the world. Stoics seem to emphasize self-affirmation and especially
self-control, but in the end, this individual achievement leads to our
identification with nature or the cosmos, and it inspires a kind of impersonal joy.

Pierre Hadot points out that like the Epicureans, the Stoics focused
much of their attention on the importance of living in the present moment and making the most of existence here and now. The past is over
and done with, the future is not real, and in any case, we cannot control
what will happen days or even years from now. But we can choose to
cultivate the present and experience its inner richness—or the depth of
existence—instead of just treating it as a stepping-stone to the future.
As he explains, ancient philosophers affirmed the absolute value of
living in the present moment as a way of encountering eternity:

> Philosophy in antiquity was an exercise practiced at each instant. It
> invites us to concentrate on each instant of life, to become aware of the
> infinite value of each present moment, once we have replaced it within

the perspective of the cosmos. The exercise of wisdom entails a cosmic dimension. Whereas the average person has lost touch with the world, and does not see the world qua world, but rather treats the world as a means of satisfying his desires, the sage never ceases to have the whole constantly present to mind. He thinks and acts within a cosmic perspective. He has the feeling of belonging to a whole, which goes beyond the limits of his individuality. [9]

For the Stoic, and the Epicurean, it is the imminence of death which gives the present moment its value. As Hadot puts it, "We must live each day with a consciousness so acute, and an attention so intense, that we can say to ourselves each evening: 'I have lived; I have actualized my life, and have had all that I could expect from life.'" [10] Or in the words of Seneca, "He has peace of mind who has lived his entire life every day." [11] One incident of happiness is equivalent to an eternity of happiness, for the instant grants us access to the totality of the universe, and joy is the inevitable response to this profound experience. Indeed, it is the sign that we have achieved complete harmony with nature or the cosmos itself. And this is not just a "subjective" response, but the final coincidence of the self with ultimate reality and meaning.

In this way, the Stoics project a spiritual goal that remains significant and meaningful for contemporary life, regardless of our religious affiliation or lack of it. Spirituality is an attitude toward the world, which cherishes it and values it for its own sake. But at the same time, spirituality is also directed toward a goal—an outcome, a distinction—that makes sense of our ordinary spiritual longing by showing how certain experiences can justify our life, even in the absence of religious consolation or knowledge concerning the future. For most of us, these experiences may be few and far between, and they are the result of exceptional encounters of one kind or another. But the Stoic sage was supposed to remain in this exalted state. Of course, the Stoics admit that, with the possible exception of Socrates, no one has ever achieved such a perspective, but they claim that this is a spiritual ideal which can still give some direction to our lives.

But not everyone is capable of accepting the goodness of the world, and Nature or "the cosmos" is not obviously a perfect whole as the Stoics insist. Nietzsche makes the point that we cannot assume anything about the ultimate nature of the cosmos, for any value judgments concerning the world—that the world is "good" or the world is "wretched"—are only valuable as the *symptoms* of our spiritual health:

> Judgments, judgments of value concerning life, for it or against it, can, in the end, never be true: they have value only as symptoms, they are worthy of consideration only as symptoms; in themselves such judgments are stupidities. One must by all means stretch out one's fingers and make the effort to grasp this amazing finesse: *that the value of life cannot be estimated.* Not by the living, for they are an interested party, even a bone of contention, and not judges; not by the dead for a different reason. [12]

But this still implies that a flourishing spiritual life must be well-disposed toward existence itself and in attunement with it. Spirituality involves compassion, generosity, and reverence, and all these presuppose openness and the affirmation of life.

NIETZSCHE ON JOY

Nietzsche lived hundreds of years after the emergence of the Stoic school. He criticizes the Stoics and the Epicureans at various points in his writings, and it would certainly be a mistake to think of him as a latter-day Stoic. But at the same time, Nietzsche seems to be profoundly influenced by the Stoic view of life, and some of his most important concepts are inspired by Stoic originals. For example, the Stoics affirmed the ultimate goodness of the cosmos: we must accept whatever happens as the will of Zeus, or the justified reason of the universe. Nietzsche denied that the world possessed any order, and in various passages he criticizes the (Stoic) view that the world is a well-ordered whole that can be grasped as something reasonable or good. For example,

> And do you know what "the world" is to me? Shall I show it to you in my mirror? This world; a monster of energy without beginning or end, a rigid quantum of forces, unyielding as bronze, becoming neither greater nor smaller, that does not expend itself but only transforms itself . . . a sea of forces flowing and rushing together, in perpetual flux. [13]

Nietzsche never sought to justify the existence of the world in any way; as we saw earlier, he saw value in suffering but he did not regard it as part of the overall order of things. And yet at the same time he affirmed the old Stoic doctrine of *amor fati* (love of fate) as the basic prescription for spiritual greatness: "My formula for greatness in a human being is *amor fati*: to want nothing to be different, not forward, not backward, not in all eternity. Not merely to bear what is necessary, still less to conceal it . . . but to *love* it."[14] For Nietzsche, this is the true measure of personal strength and power: to be capable of celebrating whatever happens as something that one wills, and in this way to identify one's whole self with it. Thus, Nietzsche actually goes one step further than the Stoics. It is not just that we must accept whatever happens, we are also bound to affirm it and celebrate it. In fact, he argues that since everything is connected together, the complete affirmation of one part of life must entail the complete affirmation of all the others.

Now we have already seen how ancient philosophy was full of spiritual exercises that were designed to transform the individual's perspective on the world, to overcome the everyday way of looking at things, and to achieve a spiritual awakening or enlightenment. In this context, Nietzsche also uses a variety of spiritual devices; he inspires the reader with his poetic philosophy, and he provokes us with his polemical writing style. But his most important spiritual mnemonic is the thought of the eternal recurrence, which he presents as a kind of spiritual parable:

> The greatest weight.—What, if some day or night a demon were to steal after you into your loneliest loneliness and say to you: "This life as you now live it and have lived it, you will have to live once more and innumerable times more; and there will be nothing new in it, but every pain and every joy and every thought and sigh and everything unutterably small or great in your life will have to return to you, all in the same succession and sequence—even this spider and this moonlight between the trees, and even this moment and I myself. The eternal hourglass of existence is turned upside down again and again, and you with it, speck of dust!"
>
> Would you not throw yourself down and gnash your teeth and curse the demon who spoke thus? . . . Or how well disposed would you have to become to yourself and to life to crave nothing more fervently than this ultimate eternal confirmation and seal?[15]

Like most of Nietzsche's ideas, the thought of eternal recurrence is open to a number of different interpretations. Notes and fragments found after his death suggest that he was interested in the eternal recurrence as a scientific possibility, and there are places where he attempts a scientific proof.[16] In his published writings, however, the eternal recurrence is clearly intended as a thought experiment which forces us to come to terms with our own basic attitude toward existence itself. Do we treat the present moment as just a means to an end and sacrifice it for the future that never comes? Do we live in continual regret about what has happened and which cannot be undone? The thought of eternal recurrence announces the overcoming of all established time relations, for the past will one day be the future again, and the present will recur an infinite number of times. So if we are *not* well-disposed toward existence, and if we take the idea of eternal recurrence seriously, the only response must be one of complete despair: "Would you not throw yourself down and gnash your teeth and curse the demon who spoke thus?" Perhaps when we first hear it, the eternal recurrence seems to be an expression of complete nihilism, and the endless repetition of everything without any final goal. Certainly, if we look for meaning at the end of a constantly deferred future, then there is nothing to look forward to—no heaven or nothingness that would represent the end of all our striving. And if we live in regret about the past, we must be doubly despairing because the past will return and we must endure it once more.

As in Stoicism, however, the one thing that we *can* change in this scenario is our own attitude toward the life we have been given. Hence, the second part of the parable: Can you imagine how well-disposed toward existence you would have to be to treat eternal recurrence not as a curse or an affliction but as the greatest news that you have ever heard? "You are a god, and never have I heard anything more divine." This response is one that affirms the present moment with complete *joy*. It values the present moment not as a means to an end, but for itself, as something absolutely precious and worthy of celebration. So when we hear that it *will* recur, along with every other moment, it is the most blissful thought imaginable.

In this respect, the eternal recurrence is intended as a transformative thought. It functions as a kind of test placed upon our actions now from the perspective of eternity: Do you really want to do this now? Could you live with yourself if you had to repeat this over and over again for the rest of eternity? And if the answer is no, then you must change your attitude toward life and the present moment, since there is no final escape and this moment will recur again and again, regardless of whether you want it to or not.

Now Nietzsche seems to believe that if you affirm one moment of life, then you have to affirm all of them; since all the moments are knotted up together they presuppose or imply each other. As he puts it in *Thus Spoke Zarathustra*, "Have you ever said Yes to a single joy? O my friends, then you said Yes too to all woe. All things are entangled, ensnared, enamored; if ever you wanted one thing twice, if ever you said, 'You please me, happiness! Abide, moment!' then you wanted all back. All anew, all eternally, all entangled, ensnared, enamored—oh, then you loved the world."[17] In this way, the thought of eternal recurrence becomes the key to the affirmation of life. Can you will the return of everything, including all the anguish and the pain of the past? In *Thus Spoke Zarathustra*, Zarathustra shows his spiritual strength by joyfully affirming the eternal recurrence of all things. He acknowledges the objection of suffering, and he argues that it is by no means an objection to existence itself. In the end, he seems to call for an indiscriminate celebration of life, which ignores life's cruelty and affirms suffering as inevitable and even a good thing if it leads to self-overcoming.

So *could* anyone will the eternal recurrence of all things? Going back to the discussion of suffering in the first chapter, this would have to include the Holocaust, the killing fields of Cambodia and Rwanda, and many other atrocities that have occurred in the twentieth century alone. Could anyone be capable of such affirmation? Or is the whole idea offensive and absurd? In his book, *Remnants of Auschwitz*, Georgio Agamben makes a decisive point:

> Let us imagine that repeating the experiment that Nietzsche, under the heading "the heaviest weight," proposes in *The Gay Science*. "One day or one night, a demon glides beside a survivor and asks: "Do you want Auschwitz to return again and again, innumerable times, do you want every instant, every single detail of the camp to repeat itself for eternity, returning eternally in all the same precise sequence in which they took place? Do you want this to happen again, again and again for eternity?" This simple reformulation of the experiment suffices to refute it beyond all doubt, excluding the possibility of its even being proposed.[18]

Can the suffering of Auschwitz be affirmed, let alone joyfully affirmed, from the standpoint of eternity? Nietzsche does not want to *justify* such suffering as part of another theodicy, but his goal is to restore the sacred character of the world that we have abandoned, and for him, this means celebrating each and every moment of life without hesitation or regret. Of course, some suffering is ennobling, but Nietzsche's idea of eternal recurrence seems to *require* the celebration of Auschwitz and other atrocities just because they happened.

In the end this is not a good perspective. Spiritual life requires affirmation and gratitude for what we have been given. But it also requires discrimination and discernment. The point is not to reject life as a mistake, or to affirm it mindlessly, but to show how life is spiritually significant and possesses meaning in spite of all its difficulties. Spiritual life is complex, and as we have seen in this book, it includes different modalities and forms of expression. Suffering calls out for justification or something that would confer meaning and sense, but sometimes this is not forthcoming. In fact, as Levinas argues, perhaps the only way to make sense out of suffering is to show how (sometimes) it teaches us to care for other people. There will be times when we can experience the joy of existence and our sense of belonging to nature or the cosmos itself—and this could be the apogee of our spiritual life. But at other times, spiritual life requires sacrifice, compassion, forgiveness, or other attitudes apart from reverence or joy.

In the end, joy is the final outcome of spiritual inquiry, although it is not a goal that we can strive for directly, since that would turn it into a selfish project. And in spite of what Nietzsche says, joy cannot be achieved through an act of will, even by affirming the eternal recurrence of all things. Perhaps, following the Stoics, we can prepare ourselves for joy by cultivating a sense of what is and what is not up to us, but in the end, joy is something that just happens. It is like the moment of *satori*, or enlightenment, which is completely beyond our personal control. In this respect, the very earliest philosophers had a much deeper understanding of the relationship between joy and spiritual experience, and the classical Indian text, *The Upanishads*, can now be read as the most original attempt to make sense of spiritual inquiry as a fundamental aspect of human life.

ORIGINAL BLISS: *THE UPANISHADS*

The discussion of joy as the apogee of spiritual life finally brings us back, then, to the very first philosophers of ancient India who speculate on the difference between the everyday world and the ultimate level of reality that subtends it. *The Upanishads* propose a form of "spiritual idealism," according to which, this world cannot be understood in merely physical terms, but neither is it just a mental projection or the effect of "subjective idealism." The point is that ultimate reality is spiritual in character, and if we are prepared to sacrifice our individual desires and perspectives, we may recover this absolute unconditioned level of consciousness and experience the greatest bliss, which cannot be known by those who remain completely within the everyday realm of the senses. According to this doctrine, the inmost self (or Atman) is identical to the highest reality, and everything else that we consider real is just a deviation from it. To go from the everyday level to the highest level involves spiritual enlightenment—not just intellectual under-standing—and this inspires complete joy in the sense of belonging to the truth and everything that is.

In a passage from the *Katha Upanishad*, there is a description of the individual ego and its relation to the deeper self, or Atman:

> There are two selves, the separate ego
> And the indivisible Atman. When
> One rises above I and me and mine,
> The Atman is revealed as one's real Self.
> When all desires that search in the heart
> Are renounced, the mortal becomes immortal.
> When all the knots that strangle the heart
> Are loosened, the mortal becomes immortal.
> This sums up the teaching of the scriptures. [19]

Before we achieve enlightenment, we believe that the separate world of individual beings is the only real world, and so we passionately pursue our individual desires, although we never gain lasting happiness. Like-wise, when we identify with our own individual ego, we treat others as totally separate and different from us, and so our alienation persists. But according to *The Upanishads*, through meditation and the will to spiritual progress we can experience the deeper reality of the self as pure consciousness, or Atman, which is the undifferentiated ground of our personal being. This means that in abandoning our selfish projects we actually experience the deepest truth of the world. Thus, in the *Katha Upanishad*, the boy Nachiketa rejects all worldly prizes because he realizes that such things are not that important in the context of eternity. Instead, he insists that he should be told the secret of death—for he is much more concerned about the meaning of life than worldly success or enjoyment. Is death the end? The King of Death tells him that no one is ever born or dies: birth and death are aspects of our physical existence, but our deepest level of consciousness is never born and it never dies. This deepest level of consciousness is the Atman, and it is something we share with all others. It cannot be known by reason or by sense experience, but it is infinite and eternal, and once we experience it we can look at death as something that only exists for those who are ignorant.

Another of the basic teachings of *The Upanishads* is that Atman *is* Brahman, or ultimate reality, for in the end there is nothing to distinguish the undifferentiated self from the unconditioned principle of reality itself. In the *Chandogya Upanishad*, this insight is expressed in the famous slogan, *tat tvam asi* ("you are that!"), which Uddalaka repeats to his son as the basic truth of Vedanta wisdom. But once again, it is a truth that must be experienced since it goes beyond intellectual understanding, and it is not something that is given through the testimony of the senses:

> As the rivers flowing east and west
> Merge in the sea and become one with it,
> Forgetting they were ever separate rivers,
> So do all creatures lose their separateness
> When they merge at last into pure Being.
> There is nothing that does not come from him.
> Of everything he is the inmost Self.
> He is the truth; he is the Self supreme.
> You are that, Shvetaketu, you are that. [20]

What is the nature of this underlying reality? *The Upanishads* are a sort of philosophical poetry, and they do not give us a precise account of such things, since ultimate reality is literally beyond words. Certainly, we must try to experience the inspiration of the text; but we should also bear in mind that in *The Upanishads* the true devotee often spends years with a teacher who requires hard work, as well as introspection and a complete change of life in order to achieve such insight. It seems that ultimate reality may never be given to us once and for all, but it can be glimpsed in different kinds of key experiences (including the one that Rousseau describes in the sense of complete harmony with nature or the cosmos). In each case, one recurrent image suggests a point of comparison: for just as a lump of salt dissolves when it is thrown into water, so whoever comes to this reality will lose herself in it, and then everything she calls her own will vanish. But what does remain is the complete identification with everything that is, and this can inspire an enduring transcendent joy. From the *Brihadaranyaka Upanishad*:

> As a lump of salt thrown in water dissolves and cannot be taken out again, though wherever we taste the water it is salty, even so, beloved, the separate self dissolves in the sea of pure consciousness, infinite and immortal. Separateness arises from identifying the Self with the body,

which is made up of the elements; when this physical identification dissolves, there can be no more separate self. This is what I want to tell you, beloved.[21]

This is the ultimate reality of the world, or Brahman, and *The Upanishads* insist that he who *knows* Brahman *becomes* Brahman.

According to *The Upanishads*, the most complete reality is found at the level of Brahman and individual lives are viewed as secondary by comparison. Thus in the *Brihadaranyaka Upanishad*, Yajnavalka decides he must renounce his life as a householder to find immortality through enlightenment, and he reminds his wife that individuals are not important in themselves but only because they belong to the Self (or Atman) that underlies them: "A wife loves her husband not for his own/ sake, dear, but because the Self lives in him. A husband loves his wife not for her own/ sake, dear, but because the Self lives in her./ . . . Everything is loved not for its own sake, but because the Self lives in it."[22] But this distinction does not lead to contempt for individual existence or the desire to end it. On the contrary, in *The Upanishads* all individuals belong to Brahman, and so they must be viewed as sacred. The face of the divine is everywhere in these works, and there is no sense in which *The Upanishads* could be seen as indifferent to individual existence or regard it with contempt. In the *Shvetashvatara Upanishad*, there is a striking passage which seems to celebrate the diversity of human existence as an expression of the divine; it is by no means unique, but it is especially powerful: "He is fire and the sun, and the moon/ And the stars. He is the air and the sea,/ And the Creator, Prajapati./ He is this boy, he is that girl, he is/ this man, he is that woman, and he is/ This old man, too, tottering on his staff./ His face is everywhere."[23] This suggests a strong metaphysical basis for compassion: for once we realize that we all belong to the same Brahman that supports us, then in a real sense we must see the other as another self, another fragment of the divine that belongs to the basic unity of being. We are all bound to each other, and the *Upanishads* enjoins the obligation to revere each other as separate manifestations of Brahman. This is the mystical truth of the world that is experienced with complete joy or bliss, and it is incorporated at the deepest level of our being. But it is the same reality that we encounter whenever we experience reflective joy.

The Upanishads were written at the point when reason first began to challenge the received ideas of religion. Their goal is spiritual truth in the context of rational reflection. In this respect, *The Upanishads* belong to the wisdom literature of India and they are inspired by a spiritual intuition that inaugurates philosophy itself. Like the other works that we have discussed in this chapter, *The Upanishads* show how joy is evoked by the overcoming of isolation and alienation. From this standpoint, joy is not to be viewed as a personal possession, or something we must fight for, but as a kind of happiness that we enter into once we are attuned to the deeper reality of the world. For,

> To know the unity of all life leads
> to deathlessness; to know not leads to death.
> Both are hidden in the infinity
> Of Brahman, who is beyond both. . . .
> Even as the sun shines, and fills all space
> With light, above, below, across, so shines
> The Lord of Love and fills the hearts of all created beings.
> From him the cosmos comes, he who teaches
> Each living creature to attain perfection
> According to its own nature. [24]

In passages such as this one, the devotee is able to experience complete radiant joy by identifying her own perfection with the perfection of the universe itself.

I would suggest that contemporary spiritual inquiry of every kind can be viewed as an attempt to recover the ultimate ground that the earliest philosophers described as "Brahman." And the recognition that Atman is Brahman also implies that we may have access to the deepest spiritual truth if we are prepared to strive for it. *The Upanishads* offer some direction for the individual seeker who is engaged on a spiritual quest. But at the same time it warns us that we cannot achieve ultimate reality and truth through self-affirmation or complete self-control (as Nietzsche and the Stoics seem to claim). Clearly, there are some similarities between each of the three philosophical approaches—Stoicism, Nietzsche, and Vedanta—in their respective attitudes toward joy as a spiritual outcome. They seem to agree that the most spiritually evolved people are in complete attunement with the world or the cosmos itself, and their sense of attunement provokes joy as a basic response. But they also claim that joy is a very rare achievement that only a few can reach—the Indian philosopher or the guru who devotes his whole life to spiritual cultivation; Nietzsche's overman or anyone who can affirm the eternal recurrence of all things; and the Stoic sage who conforms to the highest power of reason or nature (although it is unclear whether such an individual has ever existed!). Against this it can be said that reflective joy is *not* such an unusual emotion, and provided our minds are not too busy or cluttered, it is possible to experience this kind of joy at different times. Indeed, the goal would be to cultivate such experiences by clearing our minds and being ready to receive joy whenever it may come—refusing to determine this experience in advance, and rejecting any fixed ideas concerning what it *should* be like. In the end, all of these philosophies are in agreement that reflective joy involves a sense of gratitude for what we have been given. It involves thankfulness for the sheer fact of existing and belonging to the world. And it is exuberant, because it affirms the underlying goodness of the world at every moment.

Afterword

This book describes a philosophy of spiritual life. It follows a spiritual journey that begins with suffering and ends in joy. But there is nothing definitive about the philosophical account that is outlined in these pages. There are many different spiritual paths, and there are also many paths through the field of spirituality. And since the goal is to cultivate our spiritual life, the *best* path would be just the one which is most illuminating, or the most inspiring. We could also describe some of the basic spiritual types, including soldier, sage, and saint, or we could try to articulate the nature of "spiritual reality" in more detail and depth. And there are other guiding questions we could follow: Should we think of the spiritual realm as an objective place? Or is it better to understand it as a region of significance that gives depth to human life? Is religion the only locus of spiritual experience, or is spirituality finally independent of religious belief? By contrast, *The Heart of Wisdom* offers a philosophy of spiritual life that is focused on spiritual themes in the order of their emergence at the conceptual and experiential levels. It assumes that philosophy can illuminate spirituality, and it shows how philosophy can itself become a spiritual path. In this respect, it returns philosophy to its original "mission," which is philosophy as a way of life, and not just an exercise in analytical reasoning.

We began with a discussion of suffering, and the way it evokes spiritual reflection. Thinking is usually a response to some difficulty that we encounter, and while it would be profoundly problematic to insist that everything is always for the best, suffering, when it doesn't overwhelm us or destroy the meaning of our lives, makes us think about the big picture, and the value of being alive. After suffering, we focused on the spiritual virtues. Compassion, in particular, is the original response to others, and it involves stepping away from oneself and one's own projects in order to acknowledge the reality of another person's pain. To experience compassion is to be open to the greater reality of life, and it is both ethically and spiritually significant: for it is the origin of moral experience, and an escape from total self-involvement.

Suffering belongs to the *passive* register of human experience; in fact, it defines it. To suffer is to be trapped and unable to escape from one's self. In this regard, compassion is also a form of suffering—in fact, it is *suffering for the suffering of the other*. Another person's suffering is disturbing, it grieves me, but even if I cannot help, I can still acknowledge her misfortune. Hence, compassion belongs to the passive register of spiritual experience, but at the same time, it is also the openness of response and receptivity which is the precondition for an active spiritual life. Compassion opens our spiritual life, and it is more basic and easier than love. But without compassion, our spiritual life would not exist.

The epitome of the *active* spiritual dimension is generosity. This involves giving what one has, but also—and this is more important—it means giving *oneself* to others. To be spiritual is to be grateful for the generosity of life: the fact that we are alive to experience the happiness of the present moment. And we can embody this generosity by giving what we have, and by giving *ourselves* to others. This does not mean extravagance, but caring, which puts the needs of another person ahead of our own. Forgiveness is one of the best examples of spiritual overcoming, since it involves tearing up the accounts, and removing the weight of the past for the sake of the offender. Such forgiveness is "mad" because it cannot be understood in terms of the ordinary forms of rational life, which require a tally of gains and losses. But true forgiveness does not require amends. It is an expression of generosity, and an achievement of the active dimension of spiritual life.

Next, we considered the *reflective* dimension of spiritual life in reverence, which involves an awareness of objective spiritual realities. This includes a sense of awe and respect for greater realities such as nature, art, truth, and humankind, and the acknowledgement of their priority over us. And for as long as we recognize that they are much greater than we are, we must experience the sense in which *we* belong to *them*, and the withdrawal of the self as an isolated being. *Joy* describes the affective dimension of this spiritual attunement and belonging. People use different words—happiness, tranquility, bliss, etc.—but "joy" clearly expresses an ecstatic sense of identification with ultimate spiritual truths. From a philosophical perspective, we are bound to be suspicious of such emotions since joy can be self-induced or based on nothing. And even authentic spiritual joy may be overwhelmed by the vicissitudes of everyday life. But this kind of joy remains the expression of spiritual achievement. It is the feeling of power and strength that accompanies a sense of belonging to spiritual realities. And it marks the end of the spiritual journey which began with suffering and the anguish of personal existence.

Some readers may still challenge the validity of this project: earlier, in the introduction to this book, I raised a question concerning the metaphysical standpoint of *The Heart of Wisdom*, and what, if anything, can be assumed about the reader's own beliefs, or lack of them. In fact, this book does not have a philosophical or a religious agenda, and it does not identify with any particular perspective, such as Stoicism, Buddhism, Christianity, or atheism. I did not want to predetermine the results of this inquiry. In the course of six chapters, I looked at a variety of different views, but I did not affirm or deny the priority of any one of them, and this book is not an apology for any particular point of view. What I *do* believe is that there is a collective spiritual wisdom which different religious and philosophical traditions contribute to, and regardless of one's own religious or philosophical commitments—Christian, atheist, Buddhist, agnostic, Moslem, or skeptic—it is still possible to experience spiritual transformation and growth by coming to grips with spiritual themes that are developed by various philosophers and in different religious traditions. In *The Heart of Wisdom*, among other issues, we examined the creative tension between Buddhism and Christianity on the nature of compassion, and the convergence of Stoicism and early Vedanta philosophy on the nature of joy and the place of the individual within the cosmos. But this would have been impossible if we had affirmed the superiority of any given metaphysical claims. This is not to assert a kind of spiritual relativism. It is just to say that spiritual inquiry may be more productive and inspiring if it is not constrained by strong metaphysical beliefs that determine reflection in advance.

Today, it is not unusual for people to separate spiritual questions from religious ones—people say that they are "spiritual but not religious"—and even within a religious tradition, such as Christianity, some will be much more spiritual than others. Likewise, different forms of spirituality can coexist, such as monasticism, evangelicalism, or Quakerism, within the same religious tradition. Having Christian, Buddhist, or atheist beliefs will shape one's spiritual life accordingly. But at the same time, as this book has shown, spirituality is a realm of human experience that transcends any particular beliefs or metaphysical commitments. Our spiritual life has a momentum of its own, and this cannot be completely *determined* by what we choose to believe. At the very least, we should say that spirituality can be viewed as a separate sphere of life, and by putting our own beliefs and commitments to one side—suspending belief as well as disbelief—we can grasp spiritual realities more clearly and in a less encumbered way. The final proof of all this lies in the outcome of this inquiry, and whether the reader experiences the spiritual transformation that we have described as "the way of philosophy."

At this point, we can return to the relationship between philosophy and spirituality as two related perspectives that allow us to open the heart of wisdom. Philosophy is a way of life that is concerned with living wisely, and reflection on spiritual themes is the key to living well. Spirituality requires rational reflection in order to articulate spiritual attitudes. But at the same time, spirituality cannot be limited to intellectual views. It involves understanding, but it also includes spiritual practices and spiritual exercises which lead to the incorporation of spiritual ideas at the deepest level of our being. In this respect, spirituality and philosophy—or spiritual philosophy—lies at the heart of wisdom. Perhaps for some, spirituality is instinctual, intuitive, and automatic. Others trust the religious parameters of spirituality and this provides the outline of the spiritual journey they are meant to undergo. But for those who are the intended readers of this book, *the way of philosophy* is the key to an authentic spiritual life.

Recommended Reading

INTRODUCTION

Some books that look at spirituality from a philosophical perspective:

Comte-Sponville, Andre. *The Little Book of Atheist Spirituality*. Translated by N. Huston. New York: Viking, 2006.
Cottingham, John. *The Spiritual Dimension: Religion, Philosophy and Human Value*. Cambridge: Cambridge University Press, 2005.
McGhee, Michael, ed. *Philosophy, Religion and the Spiritual Life*. Cambridge: Cambridge University Press, 1992.
Solomon, Robert. *Spirituality for the Skeptic*. Oxford: Oxford University Press, 2002.

Some books that examine philosophy as a way of life:

Ferry, Luc. *What Is the Good Life?* Translated by L. Cochrane. Chicago: University of Chicago Press, 2005.
Foucault, Michel. *The Use of Pleasure*. Translated by Robert Hurley. New York: Random House, 1986.
Hadot, Pierre. *Philosophy as a Way of Life*. Translated by M. Chase. Oxford: Blackwell, 1995.
———. *What Is Ancient Philosophy?* Translated by M. Chase. Cambridge: Harvard, 2002.

1. SUFFERING

Améry, Jean. *At the Mind's Limits*. Bloomington: Indiana University Press, 1980.
Book of Job. Translated by S. Mitchell. New York: Harper, 1992.
Bowker, John. *Problems of Suffering in Religions of the World*. Cambridge: Cambridge University Press, 1970.

Epictetus. *The Handbook*. Translated by N. White. Indianapolis: Hackett, 1983.
Levinas, Emmanuel. *Collected Philosophical Papers*. Translated by A. Lingis. Pittsburgh: Duquesne University Press, 1998.
Levinas, Emmanuel. *Time and the Other*. Translated by R. Cohen. Pittsburgh: Duquesne University Press, 1987.
Nietzsche, Friederich. *Beyond Good and Evil*. Translated by W. Kaufmann. New York: Vintage, 1966.
Scarry, Elaine. *The Body in Pain*. Oxford: Oxford University Press, 1985.
Vetlesen, Arne. *A Philosophy of Pain*. Translated by J. Irons. London: Reaktion, 2009.

2. COMPASSION

Aquinas, Thomas. *Summa Theologiae*, vol. 34. London: Blackfriars, 1995.
Armstrong, Karen. *Twelve Steps to a Compassionate Life*. New York: Knopf, 2010.
Batchelor, Stephen. *Buddhism without Beliefs*. New York: Riverhead, 1997.
Dalai Lama, *Ethics for the New Millennium*. New York: Riverhead, 1999.
———. *How to Expand Love*. New York: Atria, 2005.
Davidson, Richard, and Ann Harrington, eds. *Visions of Compassion*. Oxford: Oxford University Press, 2002.
Nietzsche, Friederick. *The Antichrist*. In *The Portable Nietzsche*. Translated by W. Kaufmann. London: Chatto, 1971.
Phillips, Adam, and Barbara Taylor. *On Kindness*. New York: Picador, 2009.
Shantideva. *The Way of the Bodhisattva*. Boston: Shambhala, 2003.
Tudor, Steven. *Compassion and Remorse*. Leuven: Peeters, 2001.

3. GENEROSITY

Aristotle. *Ethics*. Translated by J. Thompson. London: Penguin, 1976.
Bayley, John. *Elegy for Iris*. New York: Picador, 1999.
Kupfer, Joseph. "Generosity of Spirit." In *Journal of Value Inquiry* 32 (1998): 357–368.
Nietzsche, Friederich. *Thus Spoke Zarathustra*. In *The Portable Nietzsche*. Translated by W. Kaufmann. London: Chatto, 1971.
Noddings, Nel. *Caring*. Berkeley: University of California Press, 1986.
———. *Starting at Home: Caring and Social Policy*. Berkeley: University of California Press, 2002.

4. FORGIVENESS

Butler, Joseph. *Fifteen Sermons*. Reprint ed. London: Tegg, 1841.
Derrida, Jacques. *On Forgiveness and Cosmopolitanism*. Translated by M. Dooley and M. Hughes. London: Routledge, 2002.
Enright, Richard. *Forgiveness Is a Choice*. Washington D.C.: American Psychological Association, 2001.
Griswold, Charles. *Forgiveness: A Philosophical Exploration*. Cambridge: Cambridge University Press, 2007.
Holloway, Richard. *On Forgiveness*. Edinburgh: Canongate, 2002.
Lomax, Eric. *The Railway Man*. New York: Vintage, 1996.

Schimmel, Solomon. *Wounds Not Healed by Time*. Oxford: Oxford University Press, 2002.
Wiesenthal, Simon. *The Sunflower: On the Possibilities and Limits of Forgiveness*. NewYork: Schocken, 1998.

5. REVERENCE

Buber, Martin. *I and Thou*. Translated by W. Kaufmann. New York: Simon and Schuster, 1996.
Confucius. *Analects*. Translated by D. Lau. London: Penguin, 1984.
Kant, *The Metaphysics of Morals*. Translated by Mary Gregor. Cambridge: Cambridge University Press, 1991.
Lyotard, Jean-Francois, *The Inhuman*. Translated by G. Bennington and R. Bowlby. Stanford: Stanford University Press, 1993.
Woodruff, Paul. *Reverence: Renewing a Forgotten Virtue*. Oxford: Oxford University Press, 2002.

6. JOY

Dasgupta, Surendranath. *Indian Idealism*. Cambridge: Cambridge University Press, 1962.
Nietzsche. *The Gay Science*. Translated by W. Kaufmann. New York: Vintage, 1974.
Rousseau, Jean-Jacques. *Reveries of the Solitary Walker*. Translated by P. France. Harmondsworth: Penguin, 1979.
Seneca. *Epistles 1–65*. Translated by R. Gummere. Cambridge: Harvard University Press, 1992.
The Upanishads. Translated by E. Easwaran. Tomales: Nilgiri Press, 1987.

Notes

INTRODUCTION

1. Friederich Nietzsche, *Thus Spoke Zarathustra*, in *The Portable Nietzsche,* trans. W. Kaufmann (London: Chatto, 1971), 436.
2. Plato, *Republic,* trans. Allan Bloom (New York: Basic Books, 1968), 193.
3. Pema Chödrön, *The Places That Scare You: A Guide to Fearlessness in Difficult Times* (Boston: Shambhala, 2001), 55.
4. *The Upanishads,* trans. E. Easwaran (Tomales: Nilgiri Press, 1987), 184–185.
5. Carter Phipps, "Self-Acceptance or Ego Death," in *What Is Enlightenment?* no.17, 38, cited by Jennifer Rindfleish in "The Death of the Ego in East-Meets-West Spirituality: Diverse Views from Prominent Authors," in *Zygon* vol. 42, no. 1 (March, 2007).
6. Pierre Hadot, *Philosophy as a Way of Life*, trans. Michael Chase (Oxford: Basil Blackwell, 1995), 104.
7. Hadot, *Philosophy,* 265.
8. Hadot, *Philosophy,* 83.
9. Hadot, *Philosophy,* 83.
10. Friederich Nietzsche, *Untimely Meditations*, trans. R.J. Hollingdale (Cambridge: Cambridge University Press, 1983), 3rd essay, sec. 8, 194.
11. John 15:13: (KJV).
12. Friedrich Nietzsche, *Twilight of the Idols*, in *The Portable Nietzsche,* trans. W. Kaufmann (London: Chatto, 1971), 511.

1. SUFFERING

1. Epicurus, *The Hellenistic Philosophers* in A.A. Long and D.N. Sedley, vol. 1 (Cambridge: Cambridge University Press, 1987), 155.
2. 1 Peter 4: 12–14: (New English Bible).

3. Shantideva, *The Way of the Bodhisattva* (Boston: Shambhala, 2003), 169–170.

4. Friederich Nietzsche, *Twilight of the Idols*, in *The Portable Nietzsche*, ed. Kaufmann (London: Chatto, 1971), 467; Soren Kierkegaard, *Upbuilding Discourses in Various Spirits*, ed. Hong (Princeton: Princeton University Press, 2009), 248.

5. Emmanuel Levinas, "Useless Suffering," in *The Provocation of Levinas*, ed. R. Bernasconi and D. Wood (London: Routledge, 1988), 163.

6. Richard Cohen, "What Good is the Holocaust?" *Philosophy Today* (Summer 1999): 176.

7. Emmanuel Levinas, *Time and the Other*, trans. R. Cohen (Pittsburgh: Duquesne University Press, 1987), 69.

8. Eliot Deutsch, *Religion and Spirituality* (New York: SUNY Press, 1995), 146.

9. Herbert Fingarette, *Mapping Responsibility* (Peru: Open Court, 2008), 136.

10. Levinas, *Time and the Other*, 61.

11. Levinas, *Time and the Other*, 72.

12. Elaine Scarry, *The Body in Pain* (Oxford: Oxford University Press, 1985), 49.

13. Levinas, *Time and the Other*, 69.

14. Jean Améry, *At the Mind's Limits,* trans. S. Rosenfeld (Bloomington: Indiana University Press, 1980), 33.

15. Scarry, *The Body in Pain*, 31.

16. See Philippe Nemo, *Job and the Excess of Evil*, postface by E. Levinas, trans. M. Kigel (Pittsburgh: Duquesne University Press, 1998).

17. *Book of Job*, trans. S. Mitchell (New York: Harper, 1992), 60.

18. Emmanuel Levinas, "Transcendence and Evil" in *Collected Philosophical Papers*, trans. A. Lingis (Pittsburgh: Duquesne University Press, 1998), 180.

19. Cohen, "What Good," 177.

20. Levinas, "Transcendence and Evil," 181.

21. Levinas, "Transcendence and Evil," 182.

22. Levinas, "Transcendence and Evil," 183.

23. Levinas, "Useless Suffering," 157.

24. Friederich Nietzsche, *Beyond Good and Evil*, trans. Kaufmann (New York: Vintage, 1966), 270.

25. Friederich Nietzsche, *The Gay Science*, trans. Kaufmann (New York: Vintage, 1974), preface, sec. 3.

26. Friederich Nietzsche, *Thus Spoke Zarathustra*, in *The Portable Nietzsche,* trans. W. Kaufmann (London: Chatto, 1971), 129.

27. "One can go further—and doubtless thus arrive at the essential facts of pure pain—by evoking the 'pain illnesses' of beings who are psychically deprived, backward, handicapped, in their relational life and in their relationships to the Other, relationships where suffering, without losing anything of its savage malignancy, no longer covers up the totality of the mental and comes across novel lights within new horizons." Levinas, "Useless Suffering," 158.

28. Levinas, "Useless Suffering," 163.

29. Levinas, "Useless Suffering," 163.

30. Levinas, "Useless Suffering," 159.

31. Levinas, "Useless Suffering," 159.

32. See for example, Martha Nussbaum, "Compassion: The Basic Social Emotion," *Social Philosophy and Policy* (1996): 27–58.

33. Levinas, "Useless Suffering," 164.

34. Levinas, "Substitution" in *Basic Philosophical Writings*, 88.

35. Cicero, *De Natura Deorum*, quoted by Luc Ferry in *What is the Good Life?* trans. Lydia Cochrane (Chicago: University of Chicago Press, 2005), 299.

36. Pierre Hadot, quoted by Thomas Flynn in "Philosophy as a Way of Life; Foucault and Hadot," *Philosophy and Social Criticism* vol. 31, no. 5–6: 615.

37. Epictetus, *The Handbook*, trans. N. White (Hackett: Indianapolis, 1983), sec. 8.

38. Marcus Aurelius, *Meditations*, trans. M. Staniforth (London: Penguin, 1964), Book XI, sec. 16.

39. Epictetus, *The Handbook*, sec. 1.

40. Epictetus, *The Handbook*, sec. 2.

41. Epictetus, *The Handbook*, sec. 9.

42. Epictetus, *The Handbook*, sec. 3.

43. Epictetus, *The Handbook*, sec. 17.

44. Marcus Aurelius, *Meditations* Book VIII, sec. 28.

45. Nietzsche, *Thus Spoke Zarathustra*, 129.

46. Nietzsche, *Beyond Good and Evil*, sec. 225.

47. Nietzsche, *Thus Spoke Zarathustra*, 326.

48. See Jonathan Glover's discussion of this point in *Humanity* (New Haven: Yale University Press, 2001), 337–348.

49. Levinas, "Philosophy, Justice and Love" in *Entre Nous: Thinking of the Other* (New York: Columbia University Press, 1998), 107.

50. Levinas, "Philosophy, Justice and Love," 107.

2. COMPASSION

1. Dalai Lama, *Ethics for the New Millennium* (New York: Riverhead, 1999), 130.

2. Dalai Lama, *Ethics*, 131.

3. Cited by Harry Oldmeadow in "Delivering the Last Blade of Grass: Aspects of the Boddhisattva Ideal in the Mahayana," *Asian Philosophy* vol. 7, no. 3: 1997.

4. Dalai Lama, "Understanding Our Fundamental Nature," in *Visions of Compassion,* ed. R. Davidson and A. Harrington (Oxford: Oxford University Press, 2002), 73.

5. Stephen Batchelor, *Buddhism without Beliefs* (New York: Riverhead, 1997), 88.

6. Thomas Aquinas, *Summa Theologiae* vol. 34 (London: Blackfriars, 1975), 43.

7. For a full discussion, see Judith Barad, "The Understanding and Experience of Compassion: Aquinas and the Dalai Lama," *Buddhist-Christian Studies* 27 (2007): 11–29.

8. Thomas Aquinas, *Summa Theologiae* vol. 34, 209.

9. Thomas Aquinas, *Summa Theologiae* vol. 34, 211.

10. Thomas Aquinas, *Summa Theologiae* vol. 34, 213.

11. Thomas Aquinas, *Summa Theologiae* vol. 34, 221.

12. Thomas Aquinas, *Summa Theologiae* vol. 34, 63.

13. Luke 10:30–35 (RSV).

14. Primo Levi, *Survival in Auschwitz,* trans. S. Woolf (New York: Collier, 1973), 111.

15. Elaine Scarry, *The Body in Pain* (Oxford: Oxford University Press, 1985), 21.

16. Friederich Nietzsche, *The Antichrist*, in *The Portable Nietzsche*, trans. W. Kaufmann (London: Chatto, 1971), 573.

17. Seneca, "On Mercy," in *Seneca's Moral and Political Essays*, ed. J. Cooper and J. Procope (Cambridge: Cambridge University Press, 1995), 162.

18. Immanuel Kant, *Groundwork of the Metaphysics of Morals*, trans. H. Paton (Barnes and Noble: New York, 1967), 66.

19. Immanuel Kant, *Anthropology from a Pragmatic Point of View*, trans. V. Dowdell (Carbondale: Southern Illinois University Press, 1978), 158.

20. Immanuel Kant, *The Metaphysics of Morals*, trans. M. Gregor (Cambridge: Cambridge University Press, 1991), 250.

21. Nietzsche, *The Antichrist*, 573.

22. Dalai Lama, *Ethics*, 119.

23. Dalai Lama, *Ethics*, 129–130.

24. Dalai Lama, *How to Expand Love* (New York: Atria, 2005), 135.

25. Dalai Lama, *Ethics*, 124.

26. Dalai Lama, *How to Expand Love*, 144.

27. Dalai Lama, *Ethics*, 74.

28. Stephen Batchelor, *Buddhism without Beliefs*, 89.

3. GENEROSITY

1. See, for example, Heidegger, *The Piety of Thinking*, trans. J. Hart and J. Maraldo (Bloomington: Indiana University Press, 1977).

2. For an excellent discussion, see Joseph Kupfer, "Generosity of Spirit," *Journal of Value Inquiry* vol. 32 (1998): 357–368.

3. Aristotle, *Ethics*, trans. J.A.K. Thomson (London: Penguin, 1976), 143.

4. Aristotle, *Ethics*, 143.

5. Aristotle complains that the community suffers when money is pursued for its own sake and huge fortunes are amassed. See Aristotle, *Politics*, in *The Basic Works of Aristotle*, ed. R. McKeown (New York: Random House, 1941), 1295b.14.

6. Aristotle, *Ethics*, 157–158.

7. Aristotle, *Ethics*, 154.

8. Aristotle, *Ethics*, 155.

9. Aristotle, *Ethics*, 157.

10. Friederich Nietzsche, *Thus Spoke Zarathustra*, in *The Portable Nietzsche*, trans. W. Kaufmann (London: Chatto, 1971), 127.

11. Nietzsche, *Thus Spoke Zarathustra*, 186–187.

12. Nietzsche, *Thus Spoke Zarathustra*, 188.

13. Friederich Nietzsche, *The Gay Science*, trans. W. Kaufmann (New York: Random House, 1974), sec. 337.

14. Nietzsche, *Thus Spoke Zarathustra*, 122.

15. Nietzsche, *Thus Spoke Zarathustra*, 190.

16. Friederich Nietzsche, *Beyond Good and Evil*, trans. W. Kaufmann (New York: Random House, 1966), sec. 295.

17. See Plato, *Symposium*, in *Collected Dialogues of Plato*, ed. E. Hamilton and H. Cairns (Princeton: Princeton University Press, 1961), 215d ff.

18. Nietzsche, *The Gay Science*, sec. 364.

19. See Nietzsche, *Human, All-Too Human*, trans. R. Hollingdale (Cambridge: Cambridge University Press, 1986), vol. 2, sec. 75.

20. See Nel Noddings, *Caring* (Berkeley: University of California Press, 1986), 11–31; Nel Noddings, *Starting at Home: Caring and Social Policy* (Berkeley: University of California Press, 2002), 13–19; Simone Weil, *Waiting for God*, trans. E. Craufurd (New York: Harper, 2001), 57–66; Iris Murdoch, *The Sovereignty of Good* (London: Routledge, 1970), 1–44.

21. Noddings, *Starting at Home*, 14.

22. Simone Weil cited by Noddings in *Starting at Home*, 15.

23. Noddings, *Caring*, 30.

24. See Freud, "On Narcissism," in *The Freud Reader*, ed. P. Gay (New York: Norton, 1989), 545–561.

25. Noddings, *Caring*, 176.

26. See, for example, Paul Monette, *Borrowed Time: An AIDS Memoir* (New York: Harcourt Brace, 1990). In this book, the author describes caring for a partner with AIDS.
27. John Bayley, *Elegy for Iris* (New York: Picador, 1999), 49.
28. Bayley, *Elegy for Iris*, 267–268.
29. Bayley, *Elegy for Iris*, 232–233.
30. Bayley, *Elegy for Iris*, 169.
31. Noddings, *Caring*, 43.
32. Noddings, *Starting at Home*, 31.

4. FORGIVENESS

1. See the chapter "Resentments" in Jean Améry, *At the Mind's Limits* (Bloomington: Indiana University Press, 1980), 62–81.
2. Jean Améry in Simon Wiesenthal, *The Sunflower: On the Possibilities and Limits of Forgiveness* (New York: Schocken, 1998), 106–108.
3. Joseph Butler, *Fifteen Sermons*, Sermon IX, anglicanhistory.org/butler/rolls/09.html. Accessed October 4, 2012.
4. See Hannah Arendt, *The Human Condition* (Chicago: University of Chicago Press, 1958); Simone Weil, *The Simone Weil Reader,* ed. G. Panichas (New York: McKay, 1977); Julia Kristeva, "Forgiveness: An Interview," *Proceedings of the Modern Language Association* 117.2 (March 2002): 296–323. See below for Derrida.
5. Derrida, "On Forgiveness," in "*On Forgiveness and Cosmopolitanism,*" trans. M. Dooley and M. Hughes (London: Routledge, 2002); Derrida, "To Forgive: The Unforgivable and the Imprescriptible," in *Questioning God*, ed. J. Caputo et al. (Bloomington: Indiana University Press, 2001), 21–72.
6. Derrida, "To Forgive," 53.
7. Derrida, "On Forgiveness," 44.
8. Derrida, "On Forgiveness," 32.
9. Luke 23:34 (RSV).
10. Mt 18:22 (RSV).
11. See John Caputo, *The Weakness of God* (Bloomington: Indiana University Press, 2006), 208–235.
12. See John Caputo et al. (eds.), *God, the Gift and Postmodernism* (Bloomington: Indiana University Press, 1999).
13. John Caputo, *On Religion* (London: Routledge, 2001), 35.
14. See Genesis 37:1–50:26 (RSV).
15. Derrida, "On Forgiveness," 49.
16. Cited in "Amy's Story—CBS News," www.cbsnews.com/2100-500164_162-165933.html. Accessed October 4, 2012.
17. D. Kraybill et al., "The Amish Way of Forgiveness," newsweek.washingtonpost.com/onfaith/guestvoices/2010/03/the_amish_way_of_forgiveness.html. Accessed October 4, 2012.
18. Dalai Lama, *Ethics for the New Millennium* (New York: Riverhead Books, 1999), 102.
19. Berel Lang, "Two Concepts of Forgiveness," in *The Future of the Holocaust* (Ithaca: Cornell University Press, 1999), 136.
20. Derrida, "On Forgiveness," 51.
21. See Susan Suleiman, *Crises of Memory and the Second World War* (Cambridge: Harvard University Press, 2006), 215–232.

22. Neil Biggar, "Forgiving Enemies in Ireland," *Journal of Religious Ethics* vol. 36, no. 4 (2008): 561.

23. Derrida, "On Forgiveness," 32.

24. Derrida, "On Forgiveness," 39.

25. Derrida, "To Forgive," 48.

26. Richard Bernstein, "Derrida: The Aporias of Forgiveness," *Constellations* vol. 13, no. 3 (2006): 403.

27. Moshe Bejski in Wiesenthal, *The Sunflower*, 115.

28. Cynthia Ozick in Wiesenthal, *The Sunflower*, 216.

29. Eve Garrard and David McNaughton, "In Defence of Unconditional Forgiveness," *Proceedings of the Aristotelian Society* vol. 103 (2003): 39.

30. Derrida, "On Forgiveness," 39.

31. Derrida, "To Forgive," 48.

32. Niva Arav, "To Exceed the Scene of Economy," in *Forgiveness: Probing the Boundaries*, ed. S. Bloch-Schulman and D. White (Oxford: Inter-Disciplinary Press, 2009), 55.

33. Derrida, "On Forgiveness," 32.

34. Hannah Arendt, *The Human Condition*, 241.

35. Hannah Arendt, *The Human Condition*, 241.

36. Richard Enright, *Forgiveness Is a Choice* (Washington D.C.: American Psychological Association, 2001), 6.

37. Derrida, "On Forgiveness," 59.

38. See Charles Griswold, *Forgiveness: A Philosophical Exploration* (Cambridge: Cambridge University Press, 2007), 95–98.

39. Eric Lomax, *The Railway Man* (New York: Vintage, 1996), 276.

5. REVERENCE

1. Immanuel Kant, *Critique of Practical Reason*, trans. L. Beck (Indianapolis: Bobbs Merrill, 1959), 89.

2. Immanuel Kant, *The Metaphysics of Morals*, trans. M. Gregor (Cambridge: Cambridge University Press, 1991), 231.

3. Immanuel Kant, *Critique of Judgment*, trans. J. Meredith (Oxford: Oxford University Press, 1982) 110–111.

4. Karen Armstrong, *Twelve Steps to a Compassionate Life* (New York: Knopf, 2010), 42.

5. Paul Woodruff, *Reverence: Renewing a Forgotten Virtue* (Oxford: Oxford University Press, 2002), 8.

6. Plato, *Apology*, in *The Last Days of Socrates*, trans. H. Tredennick (London: Penguin, 1993) 51–52.

7. Woodruff, *Reverence*, 190.

8. Confucius, *Analects*, trans. D. Lau (London: Penguin, 1984), 112.

9. "Man regarded as a person, that is, as the subject of a morally practical reason, is exalted above any price; for as a person (*homo noumenon*) he is not to be valued merely as a means to the ends of others or even to his own ends, but as an end in himself, that is, he possesses a dignity (an absolute inner worth) by which he exacts respect for himself from all other rational beings in the world." Kant, *Metaphysics of Morals*, 230.

10. Kant, *Metaphysics of Morals*, 259.

11. Martin Buber, *I and Thou*, trans. W. Kaufmann (New York; Simon and Schuster, 1996), 25.

12. Buber, *I and Thou*, 53–54.

13. Buber, *I and Thou*, 62.

14. Buber, *I and Thou*, 62.

15. Buber, *I and Thou*, 66.

16. Buber, *I and Thou*, 69.

17. Buber, *I and Thou*, 85.

18. Buber, *I and Thou*, 123.

19. Buber, *I and Thou*, 15–159.

20. Friederich Nietzsche, *The Gay Science*, trans. W. Kaufmann (New York: Vintage, 1974), sec. 343.

21. See J.F. Lyotard, *The Inhuman*, trans. G. Bennington and R. Bowlby (Stanford: Stanford University Press, 1993).

22. J.F. Lyotard, "Can Thought Go On without a Body?" in *The Inhuman*, 8–23.

23. See Descartes, *Discourse on Method*, trans. D. Cress (Hackett: Indianapolis, 1998), Part 5, 33.

24. Lyotard, "Can Thought Go On?" 11.

25. Lyotard, "Can Thought Go On?" 14.

26. Lyotard, "Can Thought Go On?" 17.

27. Lyotard, "Can Thought Go On?" 17.

28. Lyotard, "Can Thought Go On?" 18.

29. Lyotard, "Can Thought Go On?" 18.

30. Lyotard, "Can Thought Go On?" 19.

31. Lyotard, "Can Thought Go On?" 20.

32. Lyotard, "Can Thought Go On?" 21–22.

33. See Heidegger, "Exposition of the Question of the Meaning of Being," in *Being and Time*, trans. J. Macquarrie and E. Robinson (New York: Harper and Row, 1962), 21–35.

6. JOY

1. Rousseau, *Reveries of the Solitary Walker*, trans. P. France (Harmondsworth: Penguin, 1979), 88.

2. Rousseau, *Reveries*, 89.

3. Seneca, "Letter LV," in *Letters from a Stoic*, trans. R. Campbell (London: Penguin, 1969), 107.

4. Epictetus, *The Handbook*, trans. N. White (Indianapolis: Hackett, 1983), sec. 1, 11.

5. Seneca, "23rd Letter," en.wikisource.org/wiki/Moral_letters_to_Lucilius/Letter_23, 1. Accessed October 4, 2012.

6. Seneca, "23rd Letter," 1.

7. Seneca, "On the Happy Life," in *Seneca's Moral Essays*, vol. 2, trans. J. Basore (Cambridge: Harvard University Press, 1935), 109.

8. Seneca, "On the Happy Life," 109–111.

9. Pierre Hadot, *Philosophy as a Way of Life*, trans. A. Davidson (Oxford: Blackwell, 1995), 273.

10. Hadot, *Philosophy*, 229.

11. Seneca, quoted by Hadot, *Philosophy*, 229.

12. Friederich Nietzsche, *Twilight of the Idols*, in *The Portable Nietzsche*, ed. W. Kaufmann (London: Chatto, 1971), 474.

13. Friederich Nietzsche, *The Will to Power*, trans. W. Kaufmann and R. Hollingdale (Vintage: New York, 1967), sec.1067.

14. Friederich Nietzsche, *Ecce Homo*, trans. W. Kaufmann (New York: Vintage, 1969), 258.

15. Friederich Nietzsche, *The Gay Science*, trans. W. Kaufmann (New York: Vintage, 1974), sec. 341.

16. On this point, see W. Kaufmann, *Nietzsche: Philosopher, Psychologist, Antichrist* (Princeton: Princeton University Press, 1968), 316–333.

17. Friederich Nietzsche, *Thus Spoke Zarathustra*, in *The Portable Nietzsche*, trans. W. Kaufmann (London: Chatto, 1971), 435.

18. Giorgio Agamben, *Remnants of Auschwitz*, trans. D. Heller-Roazen (New York: Zone Books, 1999), 99.

19. "Katha Upanishad," in *The Upanishads*, trans. E. Easwaran (Tomales: Nilgiri Press, 1987), 96–97.

20. "Chandogya Upanishad," in *The Upanishads*, 184–185.

21. "Brihadaranyaka Upanishad," in *The Upanishads*, 38.

22. "Brihadaranyaka Upanishad," in *The Upanishads*, 36.

23. "Shvetashvatara Upanishad," in *The Upanishads*, 225.

24. "Shvetashvatara Upanishad," in *The Upanishads*, 228.

Index